THE PENTATEUCH

VINDICATED

FROM

THE ASPERSIONS OF BISHOP COLENSO,

BY

WILLIAM HENRY GREEN,

PROFESSOR IN THE THEOLOGICAL SEMINARY, PRINCETON, N. J.

"If they hear not MOSES and the Prophets neither will they be persuaded though one rose from the dead."—*Luke* xvi. 31.

NEW YORK:
JOHN WILEY, 56 WALKER STREET.
1863.

PREFACE.

The aim of this Treatise is precisely what its title imports. It does not pretend to be an exhibition of the grounds on which the faith of Christendom reposes in adhering to the historical truth, the Mosaic Authorship and the inspiration of the Pentateuch; nor is it designed to afford a complete refutation of the objections of all opposers. It occupies itself exclusively with the recent extraordinary publication of Bishop Colenso, containing an examination of his arguments seriatim with proofs of their inconclusiveness and of the indubitable verity of the statements which he impugns.

If the book reviewed in these pages had come from the hands of a professed infidel, it would probably have attracted no attention whatever. The notoriety, which it has gained, is due not to any novelty in its arguments, or speciousness in its objections, nor to any special merit in the mode of their presentation, but solely to the fact that a Bishop belonging to one of the leading churches of evangelical Christendom has undertaken to destroy the faith which once he preached. This joined with his loud professions of candour and disinterested love for the truth, his repeated insinuations of the insincerity of those with whom he was once associated, and the triumphant air which he assumes, as if confident of an easy victory, has given to it for the moment a factitious importance.

For scholars no refutation is needed; what is here written, has been prepared with the view of guarding the unwary from being imposed upon by bold assertions and baseless assumptions, and of affording those who have not the leisure for a more extended examination of the subject, the evidence that though the faith of some may be overthrown, nevertheless the FOUNDATION OF GOD STANDETH SURE.

If the author's life is spared, he hopes to be able at some future day to prepare a more extended work upon the criticism of the Pentateuch, and perhaps upon that of the Old Testament generally.

The titles of the chapters are adopted from Bishop Colenso and contain his objections in the order in which they are stated by himself. The references to his book are throughout to the American Edition, issued by the Appletons.

PRINCETON. February, 1863.

CONTENTS.

PRELIMINARY REMARKS.

MEN'S treatment of testimony is largely influenced by the prepossessions with which they approach it. The evidence of a witness, whom we know to be of excellent character and upon whose truthfulness we have every reason to rely, will command our respect and confidence. If there are obscurities in some of his statements, and even apparent inconsistencies between them, it might answer the purposes of an opposing counsel to magnify these to the greatest possible extent, to scout every method of solution that is suggested, however naturally it may offer itself, and to represent the difficulties in question as manifest and hopeless contradictions, which utterly discredit the witness. But an impartial judge or jury will be disposed to examine the matter patiently, knowing that nothing is of easier or more frequent occurrence than seeming and superficial discrepancies, when the facts are imperfectly known, and which would be at once removed if some missing links could be supplied. As long as any rational hypothesis suggests itself, therefore, by which the various statements can be harmonized, the credibility of the witness is not impugned; and even if some things should remain unexplained, his general truthfulness and fidelity will enable us to credit them.

In fact, no statement is ever made, and no narrative ever related without leaving much to be supplied mentally by the hearer or reader. Everything can be converted into an absurdity, if no allowances are to be made, nothing to be admitted which is not in the letter of the narrative, however clearly it may imply it. Such a plain, every-day statement, as that "the Prince of Wales visited America," involves much which is not stated, which is left to the presumed intelligence of every one to supply. Suppose it should be made a serious objection that the ocean lay between America and Britain, presenting an insuperable barrier to his crossing; or that the distance is so great that even if the ocean were not there, no prince would ever have consented to such a pilgrimage. And if the objector had an arithmetical turn, he might amuse us by drawn out calculations as to how far a man can swim without exhaustion, how many days this prince must have been buffeting the waves before he reached America; how many pounds of provisions he must have carried on his back to support him during this long period, and how many furlongs he must have been in height to have rested on the bottom in mid-ocean when exhausted.

If, in the midst of this tirade, any one should mildly suggest that, after all, the statement is credible, if we only assume that he came over in a vessel, such a result might be scouted as a "pure assumption, unwarranted by anything that is found in the statement under examination" (Colenso, p. 144), and only showing how "men will do violence to the plain reading of it in order to evade a difficulty" (p. 64). "The story says nothing about this vessel," "as surely it must have done" if one was really employed (p. 101). It is "a plain evasion of the distinct meaning, only resorted to in order to escape from a position of extreme difficulty, to suggest" such a thing (p. 125). On the other hand, it might be added, the author of the story does not seem to have had a suspicion that there was an ocean there, or that a vessel would be required. It involves, consequently, so many impossibilities and absurdities, and such manifest ignorance on the part of its author, that "I do not hesitate to declare this statement to be utterly incredible and impossible" (p. 114). We might be obliged to leave the objector undisturbed in his incredulity, though our faith in his sanity would not be increased, nor would our faith in the prince's visit to this continent be seriously shaken.

Now, we have no idea that anything which we, or any one else, can say in reply to the like objections which Bishop Colenso has brought against the Pentateuch will alter the state of his mind, or that of others like-minded with him. The difficulty is in the whole attitude which he occupies. He has picked out a few superficial difficulties in the sacred record, not now adduced for the first time, nor first discovered by himself. They seem, however, to have recently dawned upon his view. He was aware, long before, of certain difficulties in the scriptural account of the creation and deluge; and instead of satisfactorily and thoroughly investigating these, he was content, he tells us, to push them off, or thrust them aside, satisfying himself with the moral lessons, and trusting vaguely, and, as he owns, not very honestly (p. 47), that there was some way of explaining them (pp. 4, 5). The other difficulties, which have since oppressed him, he then had no notion of; in fact, so late as the time when he published or prepared his Commentary on the Romans

(p. 215) he had no idea of ever holding his present views. As there is nothing brought out in his book which unbelievers have not flaunted and believing expositors set themselves to explain long since, we are left to suppose that his theological training as a minister and a bishop, and his preparation as a commentator, could not have been very exact or thorough. If the Pentateuch is the book of absurdities he asserts, and these are so palpable as he asserts, and yet he never saw it or imagined it until now, his wits must have been recently sharpened, or his acquaintance with the book of which he was a professed teacher and expounder must have been limited indeed.

His mission to the Zulus, however, fortunately or unfortunately as the case may be, broke the spell. He went out to teach the Zulus Christianity, and now, at length, he is obliged to study the bible on which that religion is based. The result is the astounding discovery that the Pentateuch and Joshua are utterly "unhistorical." They are, in fact, if he is to be credited, the most stupendous fabrications and the silliest fabrications which ever were put together. How it will fare with the rest of the Bible, when he comes to apply his arithmetic to it, we cannot say. But he has threatened to carry his work of devastation into the New Testament (p. 29), and we are probably to be some day made to stare by seeing this too vanish before our eyes, the baseless fabric of a vision. Whether even Romans will be spared, upon which he has already commented in a different state of mind, and which he now commends to those who want something "to fill up the aching void" created by this sudden and hopeless demolition of the Pentateuch (pp. 214, 215), remains to be seen.

Bishop Colenso expects great results from the publication of these discoveries, for he still seems to fancy them such. His eyes have just been opened, and he expects all the world to stand agape as he has done, and to experience the same revolution in sentiment. The British church, at least, he is very solicitous to win over. He does not see why he must give up his lordly honours and his comfortable bishopric, (p. 34,) for denouncing Moses, and railing at the Son of God. He does not see why the church should not be so enlarged as to include every unbeliever in the realm, (p. 36,) who thinks with him that the Bible is at least as good as the Vedas, and that it contains everything necessary for salvation, (p. 34,) seeing there is nothing to be saved from. If this is not the case, in five years no honest and ingenuous youth will enter its ministry, (p. 37.) So thoroughly have the foundations of Moses and the prophets been shaken by this new assault. So great is the danger, which the race of bigots who still superstitiously and uncandidly cling to the truth of the books of Moses, are preparing for themselves and the church to which they belong.

We must beg leave to request the Bishop to be calm. The foundations of earth and heaven are not yet undermined. The Pentateuch has borne assaults before unscathed, and it will not be damaged by his, even if he is a missionary bishop; nor by the "Essays and Reviews" which he holds in such esteem. Colenso is not the first arithmetician who has fancied that he had squared the circle; nor is he the first who has been mistaken in his fancy.

We shall not dispute the truth of the account, which the Bishop gives us, of the way in which he reached his present convictions, nor the sincerity with which he holds them. It is quite likely that he arrived at them reluctantly, and wrote a long letter, which he never sent, to a professional friend to aid him in getting rid of his doubts and solving his difficulties. And that since then he procured copies of Hengstenberg, Hävernick, and Kurtz, of whose writings he seems to have had no knowledge before, but which he obligingly informs his readers, among the rest of his disclosures, (p. 75,) "may be found in an English translation in Clark's Theological Library, easily accessible to any one." Their answer to his difficulties failed to satisfy him. Though he has spent "less than two years" (p. 12) in examining the subject he is unchangeably convinced that the books of the Pentateuch are 'unhistorical,' that Moses never wrote them, nor were they written by any one in the Mosaic age.

He will tell us in his next volume, i.e. we may suppose, when his studies are further advanced, and he has had time to digest or swallow some of the multitudinous German conceits on the subject—"the manner and the age or ages in which they have been composed" (p. 214). The assertion of the unhistorical character of the Exodus sweeps away much of the succeeding history, but Colenso has made up his mind to the consequences, and looks calmly on the ruin he has made.

We would think better of his honesty, if the publication of this book had been preceded by a manly resignation of his bishopric, seeing he can no longer fulfil the vows made in the assumption of the office. If the Church of England is then so far gone as to reinvest him with it in his sense of it, with his understanding of the Scriptures, and after he has made this frank avowal of his belief, or rather his unbelief, he will not at least have obtained or held the position by false pretences.

With the best disposition to deal fairly and truly with him, we cannot allow the fairness and candour of his arguments. He has again and again withheld data necessary to a solution of difficulties which he is magnifying, though he adduces these very same data in some other connection to create a fresh contradiction, showing thereby that it is not innocently or ignorantly done. More than one case of this special pleading, showing a determination at all hazards to make out a case, will come to light before we have done with the book. His sweeping *ad captandum* assertions of the unfairness and mental reservations, which he everywhere ascribes to the defenders of the common faith of Christendom, do not sound well beside his flings at Hengstenberg for "a sweeping charge of dishonest concealment of the truth," (p. 69,) and that in a case where it is pretty hard not to believe it true.

However, all this has little to do with the case. The personal character of the Bishop is of small concern to us or our readers. Even as to the fairness or unfairness of his mode of arguing, he may be allowed to suit himself. All that we care about is the weight and validity of the arguments themselves. This we shall proceed to examine.

The Bishop proposes by arithmetic to overthrow the Mosaic record. Where antiquities, philology, astronomy, geology, and ethnology have failed, let us see what arithmetic can do. It is said that figures cannot lie, and yet nothing is more wofully deceptive than figures in the hand of an uncandid or unskilful man. The first requisite in order to accurate results, is to see that all the elements of the problem are present before attempting its solution. But this is prevented at the very start by the

Bishop peremptorily forbidding the admission of any thing not explicitly stated in the text, however naturally to be presumed, however necessary to the right understanding of the statements made. Any assumption required by the consistency of the narrative, or involved in its truth and correctness, is instantly ruled out. To suggest it, is to make a desperate shift to save the credit of an absurd and self-contradictory story. And the fact that such a natural and necessary assumption would harmonize everything, instead of leaving the veracity of the narrative unimpeached as most men would judge, but makes it in the Bishop's eyes worse for the author. His not mentioning it, however plainly his narrative implies and requires it, is proof positive not only that it did not take place, but he did not see how essential it is to the consistency of what he relates, and how impossible his story is without it. If anybody says that the Prince of Wales came to America, and does not at the same time expressly add, that he crossed the ocean in a vessel, his story is absurdly false, according to the bishop, and the narrator a dolt.

The Bishop, it has just been said, rules out assumptions not in so many words found in the text. But he does not always do this. We are in danger of doing him injustice. He is sometimes awake to the consciousness that words imply more than they express, and appeal to the good sense and imagination of the interpreter or hearer. He accordingly makes up for his refusal to allow what is not written in the text in explicit terms in certain cases, by the readiness with which he admits such assumptions in others. There is only this remarkable singularity in his demeanor. If any assumption reconciles difficulties and shows the narrative of Moses to be truthful and self-consistent it is inadmissible; that is a perversion of the plain meaning of the text; that is something of which there is no intimation in the story; it is a disingenuous insertion by theologians intent on saving Moses' credit by fair means or the reverse. But if an assumption dexterously made can aggravate a difficulty or create the appearance of a contradiction, he has less hesitation about it. As for example, when it suits him to assume (p. 108) that the borrowing of the Israelites was done *at a moment's notice* after they had been suddenly summoned to depart; that (p. 176) Jacob's sons brought up each time sufficient corn from Egypt *for a year's consumption;* that (p. 195) *the priests* must have been charged with slaying the passover and sprinkling the blood, on which the whole apparent force of his argument and ridicule rests, when (on p. 202) he confesses that "it is certainly true that the references to the passover in the books of Exodus and Numbers *do not appear to imply in any way* that the priests were called into action in the celebration of this feast," etc., etc.

Another element essential to the integrity of the problems he sets himself to solve, but which Colenso quietly ignores, is the general character and authority of the Mosaic record. He throws in his pennyweight, and points triumphantly to the opposing scale as it kicks the beam. But it is because he has forgotten to put in the massive weights which belong there. He shows us the difficulties on one side, as he conceives them or creates them, and leaves the impression that there are no difficulties on the other side whatever. Here, he tells us, are these absurd and self-contradictory stories. Explode them, and every difficulty will vanish. He is ready with his conclusion at every fancied inconsistency: the sacred record is an absurd story—the Pentateuch is unhistorical—Moses never wrote it.

But apart from the inspiration of the first five books of the Bible, the evidence of their authenticity and Mosaic authorship cannot be set aside by a stroke of the pen. There is such an accumulation of proof from such various sources, that the conviction which it produces is irresistible. A man might as well try to unsettle the faith of the English people in the genuineness of *Magna Charta* or prove a volume of the Acts of Parliament to be fictitious. A volume, which lies at the basis of a nation's constitution and history, as the Pentateuch does, can never be shaken until the foundations of human knowledge are overturned.

And then it has evidence of an irrefragable kind peculiar to it as a product of inspiration. The works of God evidence themselves to be such by the divine stamp impressed upon them. And the word of God in all its parts reveals its divine character and authority. Whence came the religion of the Pentateuch, with the sublimity of its doctrines and the heavenly purity of its precepts? Contrast it with the religion of Egypt, from which Israel had just come out, and with that of Canaan to which they were going. Contrast it with the religion of the most polished and enlightened nations of antiquity, and it is like life from the dead. Whence came its predictions which have been fulfilled or are fulfilling? Whence came that minute system of typical representation pointing forward to the distant future, every particular of which was so strangely matched by its counterpart fifteen centuries later? Any man who will look at the correspondences between the Mosaic institutions and the Gospel of Christ, in their exactness and their multitude, must feel a sentiment of awe coming over him. The shadows of the incarnate Saviour which are projected in fact along the whole history of the chosen seed must make him, who sees them, exclaim, This is the finger of God. The man who holds in his hands the chart of an eclipse, and notes from his own observation of its occurrence the exactness of its correspondence with the celestial phenomenon, could never be made to believe that its lines were drawn haphazard by an ignorant boor. Nor can he, who has compared the ritual of Moses with the great High Priest of our profession and the Sacrifice for human sin, believe that the former was the work of an unaided man.

And when the Son of God explicitly says, John v. 46, "Moses wrote of me," all who have any reverence and love for this heavenly Teacher, will undoubtingly receive his testimony. The utter want of confidence in Jesus and reverence for his words, which Colenso displays (pp. 30–32), is among the most painful things in his book. When a man gives up his faith in the authority and infallibility of Christ's instructions, and would not expect him "to speak about the Pentateuch in other terms, than any other devout Jew of that day would have employed," what is there left of his Christianity which is worth retaining? And yet is it not a legitimate sequence from his rejection of the mediator of the old covenant, that he should reject likewise the mediator of the new? And is it not a fresh fulfilment of our Lord's declaration (John v. 47), "If ye believe not Moses' writings, how shall ye believe my words?"

Now we would not give up the word of Cæsar, or Tacitus, or Thucydides for such a show of argument as Colenso adduces. Much less would we give up that of

Moses, whose writings are better attested, whose statements are more abundantly confirmed, and whose authority is more sacred. Our view of the case is sufficiently expressed in a sentiment which Colenso quotes (p. 16) from a friend with approbation, but which contains the severest possible satire upon his own book: "It should be remembered always that in forming an estimate of ancient documents, of the early Scriptures especially, we are doing that, which is like examining judicially the case of one who is absent, and unable to give his account of the matter. We should be very scrupulous about assuming that it is impossible to explain satisfactorily this or that apparent inconsistency, contradiction, or other anomaly, and charging him with dishonesty of purpose, considering that ours is an *ex parte* statement and incapable of being submitted to the party against whom it is made."

It is not so easy a thing, therefore, to shake off the authority of the Pentateuch as Colenso seems to have imagined. It will require more than these petty difficulties at which he carps, and more than all unbelieving critics combined have ever yet raked together to overturn it. Suppose that he has found something which we cannot explain or reconcile, shall we, therefore, fly in the face of the most formidable and inevitable difficulties? If he even succeeds in discovering some mistake, some inaccuracy of numbers (which, however, he has not, as we shall show hereafter), will it mend the matter to subvert the most certain of all history? Perhaps some day, upon the ground of the discrepancies in the army of the Potomac, which it seems the President and Gen. McClellan cannot settle within 35,000, some adventurous arithmetician will deny the fact of the American rebellion. It might be done with as much sense and propriety as what the Bishop has undertaken in the book before us.

The Zulu Bishop has also forgotten one thing of which his English common sense should have reminded him, that an argument which proves too much proves nothing. He sets out to prove the Pentateuch non-Mosaic and unhistorical. Unfortunately, his argument goes far beyond the exigencies of this demand. It proves the narrative so absurdly inconsistent that no person of ordinary intelligence could have written it with any idea that it would ever be believed. It must have been conceived and executed in the vein of Munchausen. Especially if it were a forgery professing to be the work of Moses when it was not, it would have been more dexterously pieced and less clumsily put together. It is only simple, straightforward, unsuspecting narrators of truth who relate so inartificially and leave things unexplained for cavillers to fasten upon. In proving his theorem he has only reached a *reductio ad absurdum* instead of a Q. E. D.

And then these questions of pedigree, chronology, and population, or greater trivialities still, with which his book is taken up, what conceivable connection have they with the material facts of the history? Suppose every one was obliterated or corrected, what appreciable difference would there be at last? They are petty, unessential matters affecting the purport of the whole about as much as microscopic unevennesses would spoil the stability and proportions of a Corinthian column. Suppose a doubt could be thrown on the size of Jacob's family, or some other number or date, how does this disturb the grand scheme of Providence and plan of grace which is here developed? or even the great features of the national history of Israel which are here sketched? If something of moment had been laid bare, if doubt had been thrown on some essential fact, it would have been different; but it is impossible to rise from the perusal of this book with its great swelling words without feeling that this is after all a miserable petty business, and the old fable of the mountain and the mouse rises involuntarily into one's thoughts.

He does indeed allude to questions of real magnitude, as the Creation and the Flood. Here are points which men of mark have grappled with, and which are worthy of their pen. Here is a broad border land of Revelation and Science. And the question of their possible reconciliation or hopeless discrepancy is one of vast moment, upon which great stores of learning and intellectual resources might be profitably laid out. The ground has been traversed by men of the highest ability and learning, who have not only professed themselves satisfied of the essential harmony of that record which the Creator has written in the crust of the globe respecting its original formation, and that record which he has written on the pages of his word; but have owned that it was to them one of the most astonishing of all marvels that Moses, in that age of the world, should have produced an account which without interrupting the regular progress of man in scientific inquiry, or leading to the premature anticipation of scientific results, is yet in such minute and accurate correspondence with them. The marvellous agreement in outline none can explain away. The details, it is true, are not yet settled; perhaps they cannot be for a long time to come. The difficulty is that scientific inquiry has not yet reached its last result. But where men of the largest attainments have declared themselves satisfied, Colenso, who has only begun to read upon the subject, need not cavil.

The history of his opinions on the subject of the Deluge is frankly related thus:

> "While translating the story of the Flood, I have had a simple-minded, but intelligent, native,—one with the docility of a child, but the reasoning powers of mature age,—look up and ask, 'Is all that true? Do you really believe that all this happened thus,—that all the beasts, and birds, and creeping things upon the earth, large and small, from hot countries and cold, came thus by pairs, and entered into the ark with Noah? And did Noah gather food for them *all*, for the beasts and birds of prey, as well as the rest?'"

That circumstance especially which satisfied him on this point was—

> "that volcanic hills exist of immense extent in Auvergne and Languedoc, which must have been formed ages before the Noachian Deluge, and which are covered with light and loose substances, pumice-stone, &c., that must have been swept away by a Flood, but do not exhibit the slightest sign of having ever been so disturbed."

His ability to grapple with such questions as this is revealed by the reply he makes to the hypothesis (we don't say that it is ours), "that Noah's deluge was only a partial one." Nothing, he says, is

> "really gained by supposing the Deluge to have been partial. For, as waters must find their own level on the Earth's surface, without a special miracle, of which the Bible says nothing, a Flood, which should begin by covering the top of Ararat, (if that were conceivable,) or a much lower mountain, must necessarily become universal, and in due time sweep over the hills of Auvergne."

The good bishop does not seem to be aware that the theory involves the sinking of that region beneath the surface of the water of the ocean or contiguous seas, and its subsequent elevation. This would certainly have geologic analogies in its favour; but whether true or not, the reply he makes to it does not touch the point, and merely shows that he had not the conception of the subject he was arguing about.

That the Bishop's astronomical abilities about equal his geological, may be inferred from the following specimen on p. 9. He is cavilling at the miracle of the sun and moon in the days of Joshua, and repelling as inadmissible the suggestion that the physical fact which lay at the basis of the phenomenon may have been the temporary arresting of the earth's rotation. We could hardly credit our senses as we read the Bishop's reply, in which he holds the following language (p. 9).

"But the Bible says, 'The sun stood still, and the moon stayed,' Josh. x. 13; and the arresting of the earth's motion, while it might cause the appearance of the sun 'standing still,' would not account for the moon 'staying.'"

We would like to know whether any schoolboy, who has learned his first lesson in astronomy, can beat that. Does not the man know that the moon's diurnal motion in the heavens, as well as that of the sun, is apparent and due to the earth's rotation?* We see imputed to him works on arithmetic, algebra, and plane trigonometry for schools. Can it be that his studies were arrested there, and that he never advanced so far as the study of astronomy? Even if he is not willing to build up his faith in religion on a book (p. 54), might he not without injury have built up his knowledge of science in that manner?

At any rate these glimpses satisfy us that it was well for the Bishop, and for us, that he paid heed to the maxim of Apelles, *Ne sutor supra crepidam*, and that, true to his instincts, he is content to peck at scripture numbers. We stand aghast, as we fancy over what a perplexed wilderness we might have had to travel, had he gone on in this same way through all the points of physical science in their bearing on Christian evidences, and we felt obliged to follow him. No traveller beguiled by ignis fatuus, through bog and mire, would have had a worse or a wearier time. We congratulate ourselves that he has not imposed this task upon us.

These physical matters are mere feints and side issues apart from the real assault. It is under the cover of arithmetic that he makes his deadly charge. He has no intention of scattering his fire. He professes indeed, in his introductory remarks, to have detected a vast number of assailable points, thus impressing his readers with the idea that he has sent his reconnoitering parties far and near, that he has examined the intrenchments of Moses all around, and that he could make a fearful onset upon him from a multitude of quarters, if he were so disposed. But he has not chosen to plant his batteries everywhere. He tells us first negatively what the difficulties which he proposes to adduce are not (p. 49). They are not those connected with the creation and deluge, nor with "the stupendous character of certain miracles."

We must pause here in the enumeration to say that the Bishop believes in the reality of miracles or he does not. If he does, and retains any faith in the supernatural facts even of the New Testament, why does he array the stupendous character of miracles here as creating any special difficulty in the Pentateuch? If he does not, but is here speaking sincerely, and is not throwing together a mere *ad captandum* array of possible objections to the Pentateuch, why does he say, (p. 51,) "The notion of miraculous or supernatural interferences does not present to my own mind the difficulties which it seems to present to some" ?

Nor do his difficulties arise from "the trivial nature of a vast number of conversations and commands ascribed directly to Jehovah, especially the multiplied ceremonial minutiæ laid down in the Levitical law." We are led to infer, then, that Colenso would esteem it unbecoming in the God in whom he believes to concern himself with little things. He might make mountains, but not atoms—elephants, but not animalculæ. He might make general laws for the conduct of human life, but not specify in detail meats and drinks, though he would thus incorporate the lesson that the smallest and most indifferent actions should have in them the quality of religiousness, and that in them all men should be governed by a supreme desire to please him. It is, in short, an incorporation into an outward ceremonial of the apostolic requirement—'Whether, therefore, ye eat or drink, or whatsoever ye do, do all to the glory of God.'

Nor are his difficulties such as must be "started at once in most pious minds" by the regulations of the Pentateuch respecting slavery. And here he tells us of the revulsion of feeling which these created in the mind of a "very intelligent Christian native" who was aiding him in his translations, and whose "whole soul revolted" against them. The Bishop made a shift to get over the difficulty for the present by telling him that he supposed "such words as these were written down by Moses, and believed by him to have been divinely given to him, because the thought of them arose in his heart, as he conceived, by the inspiration of God, and that hence to all such Laws he prefixed the formula, 'Jehovah said unto Moses,' without it being on that account necessary for us to suppose that they were actually spoken by the Almighty." This we take to be "the thoroughly competent, well-trained, able and pious native, who had helped to translate the whole of the New Testament and several books of the Old," (p. 217), and whom the Bishop was desirous of admitting to the diaconate without compelling him to declare that he "unfeignedly believed in all the Canonical Scriptures." It would be singular if he did believe in them with such teaching.

It is not enough for Colenso that Moses should have ameliorated the system of slavery to an extent which has no parallel in the ancient world. If he would justify his claim to inspiration, he ought to have put Israel at once under the inexorable regulations of a perfect and ideal state. He should have made no allowance for the hardness of their hearts, Matt. xix. 8; none for existing usages or the then present state of civilization. He must, if he would please his critic, ignore all adaptation of his code to the people who were to receive it, and cut off all possibility of future progress. He must anticipate the last results of Christianity working on states and empires, laws and institutions for ages; and breaking away from that course of training through which God was conducting the world, and Israel for the sake of the world, he must produce a code answering precisely to the divine ideal. How the contemplation of the geologic eras must horrify the censor of Moses, when those monsters now imprisoned in the rocky strata were suffered to range through the earth and prey upon each other and other hapless animals! How could "the great and blessed God, the merciful Father," have tolerated such an imperfect state of being for such long ages? How could he abide these gradual evolutions through successive stages, when he might have sprung at once to the completed result?

In the judgment of Moses, in which, perhaps, he is so unfortunate as to differ from the Bishop, the holding of slaves, as regulated and limited by him, was not in itself a sinful thing. The relation, limited to seven years in the case of Hebrews, unlimited in its term in the case of others, but fenced about by humane regulations and by the general principles of morality and responsibility to God inculcated in the Pentateuch, might be suffered to exist along with other hardships incident to the imperfect condition of man. He might better leave it to the force of religious principles and advancing light gradually to do it away, than attempt to extirpate it forcibly from a society not yet prepared for it. The Bishop, doubtless, since he left off his advocacy of polygamy for the Zulus, has educated himself to such a lofty pitch of morality, that all these explanations will be thrown away upon him. Slavery is an evil. Moses undertook to regulate slavery, and implant in men's hearts the principles which would ultimately do it away, instead of violently eradicating it while the hankering after it, and the state of things which produced it, still remained. This revolts the souls of intelligent Zulus, and the Lord Bishop of Natal cannot abide it.

But all these points are not *the points* on which our author relies. He goes on to swell the array of other possible arguments beside these, and teaches us still further to admire his moderation by promising, (p. 56,) to "omit for the present a number of plain, but less obvious, indications" of the falsity of the Pentateuch. And how judiciously he acts in these omissions, we learn from the reason he assigns for so doing—"because it may be possible, in some, at least, of such cases, to explain the meaning of the Scripture words in some way, so as to make them agree with known facts, or with statements seemingly contradictory, which are made elsewhere."

The Bishop, therefore, like a prudent reasoner, is not going to waste his strength in marshalling difficulties which he sees beforehand can be explained. It is the invulnerable iron-clads which are to attack the fort.

"I shall now proceed to show," he undauntedly proclaims, as he advances to the real assault (p. 60), "by means of a number of prominent instances that the books of the Pentateuch contain in their own account of the story which they profess to relate such remarkable contradictions and involve such plain impossibilities, that they cannot be regarded as true narratives of actual, historical, matters of fact." And this, though (p. 55) "it still remains an integral portion of that book which has been the means of revealing to us the name of the only living and true God, and has all along been and, as far as we know, will never cease to be the mightiest instrument in the hand of the Divine Teacher, for awakening in our minds just conceptions of His character, and of His gracious and merciful dealings with the children of men." Can any contradiction be produced from the Pentateuch comparable to that contained in the paragraphs just cited?

Note to page 24.—To prevent the possibility of misconception, it may be well to state that in 'a whole day' of twelve hours during which the sun stood still, Josh. x. 13, the moon's motion in its orbit would have carried it backward 6° or 7°, while its usual apparent motion forward in the same time is 180°—7°=173°. On the supposition of the stoppage of the earth's rotation, therefore, the moon would be 'stayed' in its diurnal course in the heavens, only an inconsiderable and to ordinary observers an inappreciable motion remaining, and that in a retrograde direction.

CHAPTER I.

THE FAMILY OF JUDAH.

THE first difficulty alleged with this flourish of trumpets concerns the number of Jacob's family when he went down into Egypt.

Genesis xlvi. 8–27 contains a list of "the names of the children of Israel which came into Egypt." These are arranged in the order of their mothers, and the descendants of each are summed up separately. The number here recorded as sprung from Leah is reckoned (ver. 15) thirty and three; from Zilpah (ver. 18) sixteen; from Rachel (ver. 22), including Joseph and his two sons, fourteen; from Bilhah (ver. 25) seven. A general summary is then made at the close, vs. 26, 27.

"All the souls that came with Jacob into Egypt, which came out of his loins, besides Jacob's sons' wives, all the souls were threescore and six:

"And the sons of Joseph which were born him in Egypt, were two souls: all the souls of the house of Jacob, which came into Egypt, were three score and ten."

Now the point which Colenso makes is this. There are two persons named in this list, and who must be included to make up the number, but who could not have been born when Jacob went down into Egypt nor for a considerable time afterwards. The names in question occur in ver. 12:

"And the sons of Judah; Er, and Onan, and Shelah, and Pharez and Zarah; but Er and Onan died in the land of Canaan. And the sons of Pharez were Hezron and Hamul."

Now if Er and Onan who 'died in the land of Canaan' be dropped from the list, it will be necessary to include in the enumeration Hezron and Hamul the sons of Pharez, or there will be a deficiency in the descendants of Leah, as well as in the total number of the descendants of Jacob. But that Hezron and Hamul could not have been born prior to the descent into Egypt he undertakes to show in the following manner:

"Now Judah was *forty-two** years old, according to the story, when he went down with Jacob into Egypt.

"But, if we turn to G. xxxviii. we shall find that, in the course of these forty-two years of Judah's life, the following events are recorded to have happened.

"(i) Judah grows up, marries a wife—'at that time,' *v.* 1, that is, after Joseph's being sold into Egypt, when he was 'seventeen years old,' G. xxxvii. 2, and when Judah, consequently, was *twenty* years old,—and has, separately, three sons by her.

"(ii) The eldest of these three sons grows up, is married, and dies.

"The second grows to maturity (suppose in another year), marries his brother's widow, and dies.

"* Joseph was thirty years old, when he 'stood before Pharaoh,' as governor of the land of Egypt, G. xli. 46; and from that time nine years elapsed, (seven of plenty and two of famine,) before Jacob came down to Egypt. At that time, therefore, Joseph was thirty-nine years old. But Judah was about three years older than Joseph; for Judah was born in the *fourth* year of Jacob's double marriage, G. xxix. 35, and Joseph in the *seventh*, G. xxx. 24–26, xxxi. 41. Hence Judah was forty-two years old when Jacob went down to Egypt."

"The third grows to maturity (suppose in another year still), but declines to take his brother's widow to wife.

"She then deceives Judah himself, conceives by him, and in due time bears him twins, Pharez and Zarah.

"(iii) One of these twins also grows to maturity, and has two sons, Hezron and Hamul, born to him, before Jacob goes down into Egypt.

"The above being certainly incredible, we are obliged to conclude that one of the two accounts must be untrue." (pp. 61, 62.)

We cheerfully grant the Bishop his premises, but cannot agree with him in his conclusion. We would not be prepared to admit that any writer of ordinary sense could so stultify himself, as he here alleges that Moses has done; not, at least, until we had first exhausted every effort for the reconciliation of his statements. We can, therefore, but repeat the explanation which has satisfied a multitude of candid and intelligent minds from the beginning and which satisfies our own, notwithstanding the sneer at those who have adduced it as willing to 'do violence to the plain reading of the Scripture in order to evade the difficulty,' and as 'having recourse to shifts in order to avoid confessing the manifest truth in this matter.'

The sacred writer evidently desires to make out the round number seventy (ver. 27) as the total of Jacob's family when he went into Egypt. In order to arrive at this result he allows himself a certain latitude of expression, which those, who are disposed to carp at words, may charge upon him as verbal inaccuracies, though he makes his meaning sufficiently plain, and no one but a caviller is in any danger of being deceived by it. Thus in ver. 8 Jacob is himself included, as well as his sons, among "the children of Israel which came into Egypt." He is also counted along with "his sons and his daughters" by Leah to complete the number thirty-three (ver.

15). And in ver. 27 "the sons of Joseph *which were born him in Egypt*," are included among "the souls of the house of Jacob *which came into Egypt*." It is plain, therefore, that the narrator was more concerned about the substantial truth of his statements than about punctilious precision in regard to phrases.

Now, including Er and Onan, the two who had deceased in Canaan, the family of Jacob, up to the time of his entering Egypt, amounted to seventy souls. Or again, if these two names be omitted, and the vacancy so created be filled up by two descendants of the same branch of the family born in Egypt, viz. Hezron and Hamul, the number will again be seventy. It no more conflicts with the good faith of this family register that it admits two grandsons of Judah born in Egypt, than that it admits the two sons of Joseph also born in Egypt, and then sums all up as "the souls of the house of Jacob which came into Egypt." The grandsons of Judah *came* into Egypt in precisely the same sense that the sons of Joseph *came*, viz. in the loins of their father, Heb. vii. 10; and in a sense kindred to that in which God brought Jacob up again from Egypt Gen. xlvi. 4, i. e. in the persons of his descendants.

But why, urges Colenso, are not

> "the children of Reuben's sons, and Simeon's, and Levi's, &c., all named and counted in like manner, as being *in* their father though not yet born?" "Why not also the great-great-grandsons, and so on *ad infinitum?*" And "why does the sacred writer draw any contrast between the three score and ten persons who *went down* into Egypt, and the multitude as the stars of heaven who *came out*, since these last as well as the former were all in the loins of their father Jacob?" See Deut. x. 22.

The reason, doubtless, is because Judah adopted his grandsons Hezron and Hamul in place of his deceased sons Er and Onan: just as Jacob adopted Joseph's two sons to be his own, Gen. xlviii. 5, 6, for the sake of giving him the double portion among his children which was his birthright, 1 Chron. v. 1, 2, at the same time declaring that this adoption did not go beyond these two. That Hezron and Hamul were thus adopted by Judah is not indeed declared in so many words, for the sacred history makes no further mention of them; and, of course, the idea would be scouted by Colenso, *et id genus omne.* But we feel warranted in inferring it, first, from the appearance of their names in this register, where they plainly stand as substitutes for Er and Onan. Secondly, from Num. xxvi. 19, where, in an enumeration of the Israelitish families existing at the time of the exodus, Er and Onan are alone mentioned of all the descendants of Jacob from whom families did not spring. There must, therefore, have been some special reason why they, in particular, are named, when other grandchildren who died without issue are omitted. Now, what more probable reason can be suggested than that they were regarded as perpetuated in the descendants of their two nephews, adopted in their stead? Thirdly, from Num. xxvi. 21, where it appears that Hezron and Hamul gave rise to families in Israel distinct from the family of Pharez, their father. But, as appears from a comparison of Num. xxvi. with the register before us, the honour of originating permanent families in Israel was confined to those descendants of Jacob who were living at the time of his going down into Egypt. The only exceptions are, first, Manasseh and Ephraim, who were raised from the rank of families to the dignity of tribes; the families or subdivisions of these tribes must, therefore, of necessity, be drawn from amongst their offspring who were not yet born; and, secondly, Hezron and Hamul.* And how do Hezron and Hamul, though born in Egypt, come to be the heads of distinct families or tribal subdivisions, contrary to the universal analogy of Jacob's other descendants? What answer can be given, or what answer need be given, except that they were, by Judah's adoption, substituted for Er and Onan, and thus succeeded to the rights which the latter would have possessed but for their untimely death?†

"But," continues the pupil and admirer of the Zulus (p. 69), "if Hezron and Hamul are substituted for Er and Onan, for whom are Heber and Malchiel, the sons

* It is scarcely necessary to remark that the tribe of Levi formed no real exception. There were but three leading families in this tribe, and these were named after the three sons of Levi, from whom they were respectively descended, Num, xxvi. 57. The families spoken of in ver. 58, the Libnites, Hebronites, Mahlites, etc., are not *distinct* from and *co-ordinate* with the preceding, but, as appears from Num. iii. 21, 27, 33, they were subdivisions of the proper tribal families, necessitated by the distribution of ministerial functions in this sacerdotal tribe, and its separation into different encampments.

† An illustration of Colenso's carelessness in argument, or ignorance of Hebrew, or both, which is very fine in its way, is afforded on page 68. Kurtz argues from Gen. xlvi. 5, where the household of Jacob is spoken of as comprising himself, his sons, *their little ones* and their wives, that, in the view of the writer, Jacob's grandsons were still young and had no children of their own. Our author replies with a triumphant air to this "feeble argument," that Benjamin is called *a little one*, Gen. xliv. 20, at a time when he "had actually ten sons of his own," Gen. xlvi. 21. He never seems, in his innocence, to suspect that the original term is totally distinct in the two cases. In one it is טַף, which Gesenius defines to mean *parvuli*, as opposed to young men and maidens, Ezek. ix. 6, as well as to adults, Ex. xii. 37; in the other it is קָטָן, which means not only *small* in respect of size, but *minimus natu*, and is applied to Benjamin as the youngest of Jacob's sons. We are strongly inclined to suspect that he only saw Kurtz through the medium of a translation, as it is the English form of expression which betrayed him into the blunder.

of Beriah, Asher's son, ver. 17, supposed to be substituted?"

We really cannot answer this. We are not aware that they are "supposed to be substituted" for anybody. If the bishop thinks they are, and will give reasons for his opinion equal or comparable to those which have been alleged in the preceding instance, we are open to conviction. Till then we will abide by our present belief, that Heber and Malchiel were born before the descent into Egypt, and are named in the register for that reason.

Here we might rest the case. The objections made to the truthfulness of this family register demand nothing more than has now been said for their refutation. But before dismissing the matter, we desire to show more fully the impregnability of this portion of the sacred record, and the futility of the attacks made upon it.

The list given us in Num. xxvi. of the tribal families, as they existed in the days of Moses, affords irrefragable evidence of the correctness and the antiquity of Jacob's family register, in Gen. xlvi.; and, on the other hand, this latter renders unimpeachable testimony to the truth of the former. We have here, in fact, two witnesses, demonstrably independent, and yet perfectly corroborating each other. The differences between them are of such a nature that one cannot have been taken from the other, nor both from a common source, nor can both have proceeded from the same hand, least of all the hand of a forger, who would not have convicted himself by the admission of such apparent discrepancies. Nor can this document, purporting to be Jacob's family register, be the product of a later period, made out on the basis of the tribal families existing when it was prepared, by concluding back from these to assumed progenitors, and hence to be regarded as an *à posteriori* construction instead of a *bonâ fide* historical narrative. For, not to insist upon the difficulty with which such a theory would be pressed, arising out of what may be styled the irregular construction of this ancient register, making all the names in some families sons, in others adding a daughter, in others still grandsons, in which it is true to the life if it records facts, but unaccountable if it be the theoretical deduction of a later age;—not to insist upon this, how is it to be explained, in the first place, that several names are found in this register to which, as appears from Num. xxvi., there were no families subsequently corresponding? There is, Gen. xlvi. 10, Ohad, son of Simeon; ver. 17, Ishuah and his sister Serah, children of Asher; ver. 21, Becher, Gera, and Rosh, sons of Benjamin, from whom no families seem to have sprung. They must, therefore, either have died without issue, or their descendants were too few to constitute a separate family, and were accordingly reckoned as belonging to one of their brothers' houses, agreeably to the principle set forth in 1 Chron. xxiii. 11. In either case their names were of no permanent national consequence, there being no representative families upon which they were impressed. How comes it to pass, then, that we meet names of this character in this register? It is a sorry shift to say that they may be purely fictitious. For, apart from the considerations that this is abandoning the hypothesis of an *à posteriori* construction, and that it brands the writer, without any evidence, with being a wilful forger of what is false, which Colenso expressly disclaims,* and which would, in fact, be very

* Page 16, note *. "I use the expression 'unhistorical,' or 'not historically true,' throughout, rather than 'fictitious,' since the word 'fiction'

inconsistent in him after the disgust he expresses at Hengstenberg for charging his opponents with dishonesty (p. 69); the notion of fictitious genealogies and dry, unmeaning lists of names is in itself sufficiently amusing. The writer's imagination or invention must have been given to very odd flights, if he thought to divert either himself or his readers in this way.

In the second place, the originality of this register in Gen. xlvi. and its independence of the list of families in Num. xxvi. appears still further from the diversity in their general construction, and the order in which the several tribes are arranged; and yet more plainly from the diversity in the names themselves, some of which have undergone considerable alteration in the long interval between the periods, which they respectively represent. When we recall the great changes which the names of many modern families have suffered both in their orthography and pronunciation, we need not be surprised that the lapse of centuries brought about like results in Israel. It is, in fact, just what ought upon natural principles to have taken place, and yet what it would not have entered the mind of a forger to contrive. At any rate the differences between these two lists are such as to show beyond question, that one is not derived from the other. A few apparent differences in the authorized English version are due to a divergent orthography adopted by our translators, where the forms in the original are coincident, as Phallu and Pallu, son of Reuben; Phuva and Pua, son of Issachar; Isui and Jesui son of Asher. In other cases the diversity belongs to the Hebrew form of the name, as Jemuel, and Zohar,

is frequently understood to imply *a conscious dishonesty* on the part of the writer, an *intention* to deceive."

sons of Simeon, called in Numbers Nemuel and Zerah; Job, son of Issachar, in Numbers Jashub; Ziphion, Ezbon and Arodi, sons of Gad, in Numbers Zephon, Ozni, Arod; Ehi, Muppim and Huppim, sons of Benjamin, in Numbers Ahiram, Shupham (Heb. *Sh'phupham*) and Hupham; Hushim, son of Dan, in Numbers, Shuham. These varying forms of the same name are nearly enough related either in their radicals or their signification * to account for the transition, which occurred in the usage of common life. But by no possibility could one list have been taken from the other, or the ancestral names be factitious, and inferred from those of families.

A still more remarkable difference between the lists of these two chapters, and one which tends still more strikingly to establish their independence of each other, has respect to the sons of Benjamin and the families which sprang from them. In Gen. xlvi. 21, Naaman and Ard are said to have been sons of Benjamin. Num. xxvi. 40, declares that the families of the Ardites and of the Naamites were descended from Ard and Naaman, sons of Bela, Benjamin's eldest son. The two accounts differ too palpably to be traceable to a common source. On the other hand there is no real disagreement or discrepancy between them. The sons of Benjamin of this name died doubtless without issue, and hence no families are derived from them. Benjamin, therefore, to preserve the number of his sons intact, adopted in their stead two children of his eldest son, naming them after the sons whom he had lost. They thus succeeded to the rights of sons born before the descent into Egypt, and each gave name to a separate family. The two accounts are

* As if, to employ an English analogy, the name of a family was changed from Pike to Fish, or from Smith to Wright, or from Coon to Khun.

thus perfectly harmonious, though drawn from entirely independent sources. And we have here again a fresh instance of adoption in the patriarchal family, which both corroborates and is corroborated by the instances previously adduced.

If now, as has been shown, the register of Jacob's sons in Gen. xlvi., and the list of tribal families in Num. xxvi. are quite independent in their origin, then the truth and accuracy of both are indisputable. Two such documents involving such a number of particulars could never agree by chance. If they are independent witnesses, and their witness agrees together, they are both true. Now, with all the superficial diversities, which have been already exhibited, these lists do in fact upon a narrow inspection tally throughout. For every family set down in Numbers, a corresponding name is recorded in Genesis. These uniformly succeed each other in the like order, with the single exception of the descendants of Benjamin, and that for a reason which has just been explained. Furthermore, the names are, in a vast majority of cases, precisely identical; and where they are not, the evidence is but strengthened by the appearance of such changes as lapse of time, constant usage, and perhaps family caprice would be apt to introduce. With its genuineness and reliability certified by such tests as these, the register of Jacob's sons can withstand the attacks of a hundred Colensos. What does all his paltry pecking at it amount to, beside such evidences in its favour? In a like case affecting the validity of a legal document, would the jury have to leave the courtroom before making up their minds to a unanimous verdict?

It is apparent that the number of persons composing a

family may be stated variously, and yet each statement be entirely correct. Everything depends upon the principle of enumeration. The parents may be included or omitted. The children of both sexes may be reckoned, or only those of one. The statement may embrace those only who are living, or at home at the time; or it may extend likewise to the absent and the departed. It may cover the first generation only, or all the descendants. A certain measure of liberty was possessed accordingly by the author of Jacob's family register, without departing from truth or becoming inexact. Omitting Jacob the number would be sixty-nine; omitting Joseph and his household, who were in Egypt already, it would be sixty-six; omitting the two that were deceased, or their substitutes subsequently born, it would be sixty-four; omitting the daughter, ver. 15, and grand-daughter, ver. 17, it would be sixty-two; and, on the other hand, including all these and in addition "Jacob's sons' wives," ver. 26, the number would have been at least eighty-two, and perhaps more. Inasmuch as one of these modes of enumeration was just as correct as another, it was within the discretion of the writer to select whichever he might prefer. He chose the enumeration which he has given us, and which yields as its total the number seventy. And there can be little doubt that he was influenced in his selection, in part at least, by the desire to produce that number.

A round number and a familiar number is always preferred to another, if nothing is sacrificed by it. This is manifest in indefinite numbers where precision is of no consequence, or is not pretended to. We speak of ten or a dozen, of fifty or a hundred. And we observe that even Colenso (p. 90) is guilty of calling the old Greek version, which according to tradition was made by seventy-two interpreters, the LXX.

It is particularly the case if a number has been fixed by usage or hallowed by association. We never speak of thirteen apostles, or of fourteen, but only of twelve. Does this warrant the inference that we never heard of the election of Matthias or the appointment of Paul? And we never hear of the thirteen tribes of Israel but only of the twelve; so that the inspired author of the book of Revelation vii. 4–8, though professedly speaking of "*all* the tribes of the children of Israel," omits one to preserve the familiar number. Perhaps, if an "intelligent" Zulu were to question his Bishop about this, he might be told that the writer was clearly ignorant of the existence of the tribe of Dan. And if the same Zulu were helping him "translate" 1 Kings xi. 35, 36, he might come to the conclusion that in the arithmetic of the Jews ten and one make twelve. The sacredness of a past association evidently controlled the language of Joseph's brethren, in saying (Gen. xlii. 32), "We be twelve brethren," although one was not. A like affection for a number similarly hallowed may have led the patriarch to fill up his family to its ancient dimensions by adopting two born in Egypt in the stead of the two who had died in Canaan; and hence that feature of the register at which Colenso so needlessly cavils.*

An additional motive for the preference of a particular number may lie in some relation of correspondence which it suggests. Thus Elijah, in building an altar in the presence of a schismatical and apostate people, constructed it of "twelve stones, according to the

* A modern parallel, as suggested by Prof. Mahan, may be found in Wordsworth's ballad, We are Seven.

number of the tribes of the sons of Jacob," 1 Kings xviii. 31. The sentence of wandering in the wilderness fixes its duration by the time that the spies, whose false report occasioned it, were searching the promised land, Num. xiv. 33, 34. Daniel (ix. 24), sighing for the restoration of Israel at the end of seventy years' captivity, is informed that seven times seventy years must intervene before the coming of the great Restorer. Matthew omits a few unimportant names from the genealogy of Christ, in order so to adjust its three great periods as to exhibit fourteen generations in each, Matt. i. 17. Such correspondences, which are frequent in the Scriptures generally, especially abound in the ritual, where all is significant and full of mystical allusions. As a single example, witness the cycle of sevens in the sacred periods, from the weekly Sabbath through the seventh month with its day of atonement and the seventh year to the highest of all, the year of jubilee, Lev. xxv. 8, 9, each in its various grade at once a commemoration and a prefiguration of that rest of God, with which the number seven was associated (Gen. ii. 3), and into which it is man's privilege and destiny to enter, Heb. iv. 3–5.

Now, at a time when instruction was so largely conveyed by mysterious hints in figures and symbols, it need not surprise us to find the suggestion of a momentous truth in the number of Jacob's family at this great crisis in their history. Nor need we be surprised that such a mode of enumeration was selected as might suggest a truth which was to be inculcated. That this is not purely fanciful, appears from Moses' directing the attention of the people expressly to it, Deut. xxxii. 8, 'When the Most High divided to the nations their inheritance, when he separated the sons of Adam, he set the bounds of the people (Heb. *peoples*) according to the number of the children of Israel.' There was, therefore, a significant relation between 'the number of the children of Israel' and the nations of mankind. The tenth chapter of Genesis, which gives an account of the sons of Noah and their dispersion over the world, makes the number to be seventy. With this the number of Jacob's family at the time when it was about to pass into a nation, when it was about to receive its permanent organization and its tribal divisions to be determined, precisely corresponded. The universal aim of Israel, its world-wide relations, which were in so many ways explicitly set forth, are here impressed upon its origin in a numerical symbol. That this number was regarded as not wholly casual but significant, and that its significance was kept in mind, appears still further from 'the seventy elders of Israel,' of whom we repeatedly read, Ex. xxiv. 1, Num. xi. 16–25, Ezek. viii. 11, a body perpetuated in the Sanhedrim.* As seventy is not a multiple of twelve, it could

* This number continued to be so understood by the later Jews, as appears from numerous passages in their writings. The following from the book of Zohar, quoted by Lightfoot, Heb. Exercit. on Luke iii. 36, may serve as a specimen. "Seventy souls went down with Jacob into Egypt, that they might restore the seventy families dispersed by the confusion of tongues."

The prevalence of this opinion further appears from the systematic alterations made in the Septuagint both in Gen. x. and Gen. xlvi. The seventy nations in the common text are distributed among the sons of Noah in the following manner, viz. Japheth 14, Ham 30, Shem 26. The account of Nimrod (vs. 8–12) is a manifest parenthesis relating to a monarch and conqueror and not the progenitor of a nation. Accordingly, his name and that of Asshur are not reckoned. If, however, these names be counted, the correspondence with Jacob's family will be destroyed. In order to restore this correspondence, while including these names, the Greek translators took the liberty of inserting three additional names in the list of Noah's descendants, viz. Elisa in ver. 2, and two Cainans, vs.

not have been determined by the number of the tribes, but must be traced to some other source.

When our Lord was about organizing the true Israel, who believed in and embraced him, he retained at the outset these numerical correspondences. He ordained twelve apostles, preserving herein the number of the tribes, and intimating that Israel is perpetuated in its full organization in spite of the excision of its apostate members. He sent forth seventy disciples, preserving thus the universal feature of Israel, and that which looked to the subjugation of all nations. But when the new Jerusalem is complete Rev. xxi. 12 etc., the twelve dominates and the seventy disappears. The seed of Abraham has then swollen to its utmost expansion, and is commensurate with the whole body of the redeemed. The nations of the world have been absorbed into the tribes of Israel. The holy city bears the names of the tribes upon its gates, indicating who alone have the right of admission within its walls. And thus Abraham is the father of many nations, Rom. iv. 17, and the heir of the world, verse 13. And the ultimate completion of the promise Gen. xvii. 4, "unto thy seed will I give this land" is something far more glorious than the peopling of Canaan to its full dimensions with his lineal descendants. It is not without a meaning that the same word in Hebrew and in Greek signifies both *land* and *earth.* So that the divine grant in its largest sense really is "to thy spiritual seed will I

22, 24; the total thus becomes seventy-five. And then in the summation of the house of Jacob (Gen. xlvi. 27) they substitute seventy-five for seventy, making up the number by tracing the descendants of Joseph beyond the first generation. Stephen retains this number in his speech (Acts vii. 14) as the one most familiar to Greek-speaking Jews, and as sufficiently accurate for his immediate purpose, being in fact strictly correct upon the mode of enumeration adopted by the lxx translators.

give this earth." All this is darkly hinted, nay, is germinally involved in this original register of Israel. The miserable quibbles, which we have been refuting, uttered without an inkling of its real significance, cannot disturb its truth, its certainty, or the fulness of its import.

CHAPTER II.

THE SIZE OF THE COURT OF THE TABERNACLE, COMPARED WITH THE NUMBER OF THE CONGREGATION.

THE second objection of our author is so peculiarly Colensonian, that we are quite willing, as far as it is concerned, to accept his disclaimer (p. 13), that he has not borrowed from De Wette in particular or the German Rationalists in general. He finds a difficulty, it seems, in Lev. viii. 1–4.

"And the LORD spake unto Moses, saying . . . . . . Gather thou all the congregation together unto the door of the tabernacle of the congregation. And Moses did as the LORD commanded him; and the assembly was gathered together unto the door of the tabernacle of the congregation."

Here it is urged that "all the congregation" must mean

"the whole body of the people, at all events the adult males in the prime of life among them, and not merely the elders or heads of the people." "The 603,550 warriors Num. ii. 32, certainly must have formed a part of the whole congregation, leaving out of consideration the multitude of old men, women, and children." "I cannot," he tells us, "with due regard to the truth, allow myself to believe, or attempt to persuade others to believe, that such expressions as the above can possibly be meant to be understood of the elders only."

He then demonstrates by a series of calculations, that

this large mass of human beings could never have stood *at the door* of the tabernacle, that they could not even have stood along "the whole end of the tabernacle" which was but eighteen feet wide, nor could they have been crowded into the entire court behind, as well as in front of the tabernacle.

We have carefully followed the Bishop through his figures, and we assure our readers that they are quite correct. If anybody has ever been in doubt before, let him never question it again, that 603,550 people could not stand in a court one hundred cubits long by fifty broad. For this is what the argument proves; just this, and nothing more. And now, if the Bishop would make the attempt, we think it not unlikely that he might prove it impossible for the Houses of Parliament, where Great Britain meets by her representatives, to contain the entire population of the British islands. And if the full-grown men of Victoria's empire were packed in solid layers, one above another, over the whole area on which these houses stand, he might cipher out the height of the column they would make.

But while honouring the Bishop's figures, we must add that as an argument to discredit the Mosaic narrative, these calculations are liable to two objections, which seriously vitiate their results. The first respects the number of people expected or actually present; the second, the space which they were to occupy.

If we turn to p. 105 of the book before us, we shall find a passage quoted, Ex. xii. 21–28, whose bearings upon this subject the Bishop ought not to have overlooked. We there read

"Then Moses called for *all the elders of Israel*, and said unto them," etc., etc.

"And the *people* bowed the head and worshipped. And *the children of Israel* went away, and did as the LORD had commanded Moses and Aaron."

And from ver. 3 it appears that this call for "all the elders of Israel" was in pursuance of the divine command to speak unto *all the congregation of Israel.*

So again in Ex. xix. 7, 8:

"And Moses came and called for *the elders of the people*, and laid before their faces all these words which the LORD commanded him. And *all the people* answered together and said, All that the LORD hath spoken, we will do."

In Deut. v. 1, "Moses called *all Israel*," and addressed them; in the course of his address, he says, ver. 23, "*Ye* came near unto me, even *all the heads of your tribes and your elders.*"

It hence appears, in spite of our author's inability to believe what so thoroughly invalidates his objection, that the congregation of Israel might be represented by their elders, and the elders might be addressed or spoken of as the congregation who were represented by them. This mode of speaking is a familiar one in ordinary life. England is said to do, what her authorized representatives or agents do. Colenso himself, in referring, (p. 34,) to "the great body of the church," feels it necessary to add, by way of explanation, "not the clergy only, but the clergy and laity."

The Bishop has given himself the needless trouble to cite a number of passages, in which the congregation means not the elders but the people generally. But the fact that in those passages the congregation is not spoken of representatively, does not weaken the force of the equally evident fact that in other passages it is so spoken of. And that this is the case in the instance now before us, is rendered more than probable by the mention, Lev. ix. 1, of the calling together of "the elders of Israel" for the same purpose for which in viii. 2 "all the congregation" were summoned; and these elders are further spoken of as "the children of Israel," ver. 3, and "all the congregation," ver. 5. Upon the most liberal construction, all that we can be required to assume is the elders and a promiscuous assembly besides. A mass meeting of the Democratic party does not mean the entire party *en masse.* All are summoned, not in the sense that all are expected or required to attend, but that none are excluded. A *town meeting* may be held, though not a fiftieth part of the inhabitants of the place are present. It has never been our good fortune to visit the city of Lexington, Ky. But as we know that Rev. Dr. Breckenridge some time ago called a meeting of its citizens in the Court-house on important business, and, as they actually assembled, we suppose that we must infer that there are not more than a thousand citizens there.

Again, Colenso's argument assumes that the congregation must have been gathered "within the court." But although this is the basis of all his computations, the court is not once mentioned or alluded to in the connection. He infers, however, that they must have been assembled within these limits; first, because they were to be gathered *unto* (or *at*, as the preposition is occasionally rendered) the door of the tabernacle, as if the crowd would not be just as much *at the door*, no matter how far back its farther extremity extended. And secondly, because they were summoned *to witness* the ceremony of Aaron's consecration. But the text says nothing of their witnessing it; still less that *all*, who were there, were to witness it, or did witness it. They might be present to signify their interest and participation in it; just as the people were without, when Zacharias went into the temple to burn incense, Luke i. 9, 10. The court was no more designed or intended to hold the entire body of the people, than the holy of holies was to contain Him who made it his symbolical residence. The small dimensions of the symbol, and its inadequacy to embrace that which it represented, might be objected to the one as well as to the other.

CHAPTER III.

MOSES AND JOSHUA ADDRESSING ALL ISRAEL.

THE next difficulty is found in—

Deut. i. 1. 'These be the words which Moses spake unto all Israel.'

Deut. v. i. 'And Moses called all Israel and said unto them . . . .'

Josh. viii. 34, 35. 'And afterward he read all the words of the law, the blessings and cursings, according to all that is written in the book of the law. There was not a word of all that Moses commanded, which Joshua read not before all the congregation of Israel, with the women, and the little ones, and the strangers that were conversant among them.'

"Now," argues the Bishop, "no human voice, unless strengthened by a miracle, of which the Scripture tells us nothing, could have reached the ears of a crowded mass of people as large as the whole population of London."

Unfortunately for the argument, this mark of the 'unhistorical' is common to all history, even the most modern and the best attested. It is natural to infer from the above that no address is ever made to the public in London. Hereafter we shall expect some reasoner of an arithmetical turn to establish that Washington's farewell address, containing what he had to say to the people of the United States, was 'unhistorical;' also that Queen Victoria never issued a proclamation to her subjects, and that no general ever gave orders to his army provided he commanded more than a thousand men.

It seems to be a pitiable thing to be obliged to repeat here such a familiar, every-day fact, as that public and formal announcements are often made without the slightest expectation that all, or even the thousandth part of those to whom they are addressed, and who are thus presumptively made acquainted with the subjects of them, will actually hear them. When the Roman *feciales* made their formal demand of reparation from a people with whom they had cause of quarrel, or when they uttered their declaration of war at the national boundary, the whole nation was presumed to be thus apprised of it. The proclamations at Charing Cross were for the English people. And what a voice must those champions have had who threw down their challenge to all the world!

And again, is it necessary to remind the bishop of the maxim, Qui facit per alium, facit per se? From Gen. xxiv. 10, he would probably infer that the servant of Abraham started off alone, driving ten camels; but ver. 32 speaks of 'the men that were with him.' We constantly speak of Christ feeding the five thousand, though Matthew xiv. 19, tells us distinctly that 'he gave the loaves to his disciples and the disciples to the multitude.' According to Neh. viii. 3, Ezra read in the law, and the ears of *all the people* were attentive; but that his single voice was not expected to reach the entire multitude appears from vers. 7, 8, where it is said that he was aided by the Levites. With such analogies one would think that no man in his senses could stumble at the expressions which have given offence to the Bishop, even if no explanation was expressly furnished. But what shall we think when we find that we are explicitly told how it was that Moses addressed all Israel, and Joshua read to them the blessings and curses of the law? Was not the Bishop aware, or did he purposely conceal the fact, that, according to Deut. xxvii. 1, Moses, *with the elders of Israel*, commanded the people, and, according to ver. 9, Moses and *the priests the Levites* spake unto all Israel? So in Deut. xxvii. 14, the *Levites* are directed to utter at Ebal and Gerizim with a loud voice unto all the men of Israel, the very things which Joshua, viii. 34, read before them.

CHAPTER IV.

THE EXTENT OF THE CAMP, COMPARED WITH THE PRIEST'S DUTIES AND THE DAILY NECESSITIES OF THE PEOPLE.

A FRESH ground of cavil and misrepresentation, we can characterize it by no milder term, is found in Lev. iv. 11, 12, where the priest is directed, after burning upon the altar the fat of a bullock, offered in sacrifice for the sin of a priest, to 'carry' the rest of the animal 'without the camp unto a clean place.' Now Colenso adopts Scott's estimate, that the encampment of Israel may be computed to have been about twelve miles square, that is, about the size of London. There were but three priests, Aaron, Eleazar, and Ithamar. Accordingly,

> "The offal of these sacrifices would have had to be carried by Aaron himself, or one of his sons, a distance of six miles." "In fact, we have to imagine the priest having himself to carry, on his back on foot, from St. Paul's to the outskirts of the metropolis, the skin, and flesh, and head, and legs, and inwards, and dung, even the whole bullock."

Our author, in his eagerness to fasten a blunder upon Moses, has committed an egregious one himself. Our translators here use *carry* as a sufficient approximation to the original expression for every practical purpose, and one which no sensible person was in any danger of misunderstanding. Colenso presses the English word to a sense which does not represent the original at all. But, suppose that for a moment we do not look behind the common version. Then we must understand from Gen. xlvi. 5, that the sons of Israel carried Jacob their father, and their little ones and their wives "on their backs on foot" in the wagons. The Chaldeans must have carried Job's camels away "on their backs on foot," Job i. 17. And in the same way, 2 Chron. xii. 9, Shishak king of Egypt must have carried away the shields of gold, and so, 2 Kings xviii. 11, Israel must have been carried by the king of Assyria. From which we infer that those monarchs must have had unusually strong backs.

It should be known, however, that all this *carrying* business is foisted into the text by Colenso himself. The word which Moses uses means simply to *remove*, irrespective of the mode, or, more exactly still, "cause to go forth," without designating the agent employed in the removal. That the removal was not performed personally by the priest is apparent not only from the consideration that the removal and burning of what was not offered in sacrifice was in no sense of the term a sacerdotal function, but also from the fact that the contrary explicitly appears, not only in parallel cases but in the very case under consideration.

In the ceremony of the red heifer, Num. xix. 1–10, which was for special reasons sacrificed without the camp, the priest must attend at the place in order to sprinkle the blood, which was a duty peculiarly belonging to the priesthood. And yet, though he was at the spot, two men were required to be present, who are expressly distinguished from him and from one another, the one to burn the heifer, 'her skin, and her flesh, and her blood, with her dung,' and the other to 'gather up the ashes of the heifer and lay them up without the camp in a clean place.'

Again, upon the day of atonement both the goat for the people's sin-offering, and the bullock for the priest's sin-offering, the latter being the very case before us, were to be burned without the camp. But the person, who performed this service, is distinguished from the priest, as plainly as is the "fit man," by whose hand the scape-goat was to be sent into the wilderness. Lev. xvi. 26–28.

Besides, it may be consoling to the Bishop to reflect, that the bodies of the animals sacrificed in the ordinary offerings were disposed of in a much simpler way. It was only the sin-offerings for the priests, and those offered for the united trespass of the whole congregation, which were to be burned without the camp. The latter would of course be rare, and as there were but three priests, the former could not be frequent. This peculiar character of these sacrifices the Bishop unaccountably forgot to mention, or else found it convenient not to do so; leaving his readers to infer, as they naturally would, that he was speaking of the entire body of the multitudinous sacrifices which the ritual required.

But we are not done with this matter yet. We have seen flaws enough in this indictment to quash it three times over; but another flaw remains to be detected, which is equal in magnitude to either of the preceding. The charge of the 'unhistorical' rests in this instance upon the assumption tacitly made, that the encampment of Israel in the desert was one continuous camp, and that to carry anything forth "without the camp," repuired a journey of "six miles" from the centre to the outer circumference. Strenuously as Colenso resists the introduction of anything not written in so many terms in the text, provided it removes a difficulty, and consists with the veracity of Moses, he has no repugnance to its being done if it has an opposite effect. We might content ourselves here with asking him to prove the continuity of the camp, which is so essential to his argument, and which he has taken for granted. And this not only without a particle of evidence, but in the face of the explicit statements of the sacred record.

In Num. ii. comp. i. 52, 53, x. 14–28, the plan of Israel's encampment is minutely described. From this it appears that there were five distinct camps. One lay in the centre, and was formed by the Levites surrounding the tabernacle, ii. 17. Then four other camps, each embracing three tribes, were distributed around this toward the cardinal points of the compass. Now, the exterior of any one of these camps was 'without the camp.' Or what conceivable reason is there, ceremonial, sanitary, or of any other sort, why the ashes of the sacrifices might not be deposited in some 'clean place' outside of the Levitical camp? but the person or persons entrusted with them, and with the offal which was to be burned 'where the ashes are to be poured out,' must traverse the unoccupied space between this and some other of the camps, traverse that camp also, and after completing his "six miles," attend to what he might just as well have done at the very beginning of his journey. If this is the way, the Bishop teaches the Zulus economy of time and labor, we admire his wisdom and their patience.

The relations of a later period may also throw light upon the meaning of this injunction. The entire encampment of all the tribes corresponded to the land of Canaan as the residence of the whole people. The particular camps which formed its subdivisions corresponded to the different localities in which the people dwelt together. But the ashes of the temple and the offal of the sacrifices were not to be carried beyond Jordan, and outside of the territory of Israel; they were deposited or burned in the valley of the son of Hinnom, just without the city walls. So leprous persons were not banished beyond the limits of Palestine, but simply required to dwell apart, and outside of the town or city to which they belonged, 2 Kings vii. 3, xv. 5. As the prescriptions of the Pentateuch are the only ones bearing upon this subject, this shows how they were adapted by the people to their altered circumstances, and of course, what they understood the real meaning of these prescriptions to be. And if this interpretation be taken as authoritative, then to remove 'without the camp' means not outside of the territory occupied by the entire people; but outside of that particular collection of habitations in which the thing to be removed happened to be.

If the army of the Potomac consists of 100,000 men, it must on the Bishop's principles be a very formidable business to remove the offal and rubbish outside of their camp. He can calculate for us what the size of an encampment must be, that can accommodate such a body of soldiers, and how far those in the centre must walk to reach its exterior limit. Before he enters, however, in real earnest upon the computation, we would advise him to inquire, whether they may not be encamped by regiments or divisions, and thus their labor be reduced, and his rendered unnecessary.

But this is not all. The Levites were to encamp

about the tabernacle by families. The three chief families of the tribe were to pitch at its rear and on its two sides, Num. iii. 23, 29, 35; while Moses and Aaron and his sons were all who were to encamp in front of the tabernacle, ver. 38. So that in order to go from the tabernacle to the outside of the Levitical camp, it was necessary to pass the tents of *these four men!*

Now, let us put Colenso's statements along side of the facts, and see what remains of his argument. The greater part of the body of a bullock, belonging not to the ordinary sacrifices but to a class rarely requiring to be offered, was to be carried not "on the back on foot," but conveyed in any manner that was thought proper, not by "Aaron himself or one of his sons," but by any person or persons they chose to employ, not "a distance of six miles," but past the tents of four men. And this is so 'huge' a 'difficulty' that the Mosaic origin and the credibility of the Pentateuch must be given up in consequence! Which is 'unhistorical' now, Moses or Colenso?

But, adds the Bishop,

> "From the outside of this great camp, wood and water would have had to be fetched for all purposes." "And the ashes of the whole camp, with the rubbish and filth of every kind, for a population like that of London, would have had to be carried out in like manner through the midst of the crowded mass of people."

Very well. There are cities with as large a population as that of London, and without its European conveniences, or its system of sewerage, as Peking for example, which continue to exist in the same place not only for one year, or for forty years, but for ages and centuries. Some how or other they manage to have their wants supplied, and their garbage removed. Could not Moses, trained at the court of Pharaoh, have directed such matters at least as well as the Chinese? His question whether "such supplies of wood or water, for the wants of such a multitude as this, could have been found at all in the wilderness," properly belongs under another head, and will receive a sufficient answer, when we come to consider his strictures upon the subsistence of the sheep and cattle of the Israelites in the desert. See Chap. X.

The objector proceeds:

"They could not surely all have gone outside the camp for the necessities of nature, as commanded in Deut. xxiii. 12–14." "We have to imagine half a million of men going out daily—the 22,000 Levites for a distance of six miles—to the suburbs for the common necessities of nature, The supposition involves, of course, an absurdity. But it is our duty to look plain facts in the face."

What is to be thought of the honesty and truthfulness, not to say decency, of a man who can talk in this manner? The "plain fact" is, that this regulation, as is manifest upon the very face of it, had nothing to do with the camp of the entire people. It is expressly confined to military expeditions. The paragraph begins (ver. 9), "When the host (the original is without the definite article, מַחֲנֶה, *a camp*) goeth forth against thine enemies, then keep thee from every wicked thing." Detachments sent out to attack their foes are reminded of their sacred character, and all defilement or impurity in their camps is prohibited. The encampment of the entire people was, no doubt, under such ceremonial oversight and had such police arrangements, as the nature of the case permitted or required. But parties on military duty away from the main body are here put under special rules, whose wisdom, even in a sanitary point of view, is obvious.

CHAPTER V.

THE NUMBER OF THE PEOPLE AT THE FIRST MUSTER, COMPARED WITH THE POLL-TAX RAISED SIX MONTHS PREVIOUSLY.

UNDER this head we are first treated to a precious specimen of the bishop's proficiency in Hebrew learning. The expression, 'shekel of the sanctuary,' first occurring in Ex. xxx. 13, and frequently thereafter is, as he remarks, rendered in the Septuagint 'the sacred shekel.' "But this," he goes on to say, "can hardly be the true meaning of the original שֶׁקֶל הַקֹּדֶשׁ." And why not, pray? The merest tyro in Hebrew could tell him, that this is quite as likely a meaning of the phrase as the other. The word קֹדֶשׁ occurs 466 times in the Old Testament. Of all these Gesenius, in his Thesaurus, finds but 23 places, in which he judges that it means the sanctuary or one of its apartments, and five more in which it *may* mean it; and in none of these does the phrase in question occur. On the contrary, he says of it, "it is used hundreds of times (*sexcenties*) in the genitive in place of an adjective;" and he adduces, as phrases in which it occurs in this sense, "holy ground, holy place, holy hill, holy Spirit, holy name, holy day, holy sabbath, holy city, holy temple, holy oracle, holy flesh, holy bread (Eng. ver. hallowed), holy vessels, holy garments, holy linen coat, holy crown, noly ointment, holy oil, SACRED SHEKEL, holy people, holy covenant."

However, Colenso may be right and Gesenius mistaken; what then?

> "The expression 'shekel of the sanctuary' could hardly have been used in this way, until there was a sanctuary in existence, or rather until the sanctuary had been some time in existence, and such a phrase had become familiar in the mouths of the people. Whereas here it is put into the mouth of Jehovah, speaking to Moses on Mount Sinai, six or seven months before the tabernacle was made."

Did the Israelites, then, pay no worship to the God of their fathers until the tabernacle was set up? Had they no divine service previous to this, and no place set apart for its celebration? Admitting that the term here used is to be translated 'sanctuary,' it involves no allusion to any structure and no implication of any. It means first, *holiness* in the abstract, then *any thing holy*, and finally, *a holy place* or *sanctuary*. The presence or the absence of an edifice has nothing to do with the appropriateness of the term. It would have been just as applicable to the spots where Abraham, Isaac, and Jacob worshipped under the open sky, as to the tabernacle or the temple. But if a building were required, has the Bishop forgotten or did he intentionally overlook the circumstance that there is distinct mention (Ex. xxxiii. 7) of a provisional 'tabernacle of the Congregation,' prior to the construction of the one ordained on Sinai? And besides when would be a fit time for instituting shekels of the sanctuary, supposing them not to have been known before, if not when contributions were making, and a uniform tribute was to be imposed to aid in its erection? That this was the origin of the 'shekel of the sanctuary' appears probable not only from its never having been mentioned before, but also from the fact that its weight is accurately defined in this passage as though it were something new; 'a shekel is twenty gerahs.'

Ex. xxxviii. 25, 26 records the payment by all the people of the required tribute of half a shekel; in Num. i. 1–46 all the people are numbered. The difficulty insisted upon here is "that the number of adult males should have been identically the same on the first occasion as it was half a year afterwards."

Colenso himself supplies us with the true answer to this imaginary difficulty, though we must do him the justice to say it is without his intending it. Listen to him.

> "These words [viz. Ex. xxx. 11–13] direct that whenever a numbering of the people shall take place, each one that is numbered shall pay a 'ransom for his soul' of half a shekel. Now in Ex. xxxviii. 26 we read of such a tribute being paid, 'a bekah for every man, that is, half a shekel after the shekel of the Sanctuary, for every one that went to be numbered, from twenty years old and upward,' that is, the *atonement-money* is collected; but nothing is there said of any *census* being taken. On the other hand, in Num. i. 1–46, more than six months after the date of the former occasion, we have an account of a very formal numbering of the people, the result being given for each particular tribe, and the total number summed up at the end; here the *census* is made, but there is no indication of any *atonement-money* being paid."

A more satisfactory solution could not be desired. Even if we were disposed to be critical, we would ask no other emendation of the above than first the restoration of the word *when*, for which *whenever* has been quietly substituted in the first sentence. The direction is not a general one, but has relation to a specific case. In no other instance in the Old Testament do we find this tribute connected with a numbering of the people. And secondly we would insert a note of interrogation after the 'six months' of the last sentence.

We have then in Ex. xxx. according to Colenso, a direction that a tribute and a census shall be taken together. In Ex. xxxviii. the *tribute* is collected but nothing said of the *census.* In Num. i. the *census* is taken but nothing said of the *tribute.* The fair inference from these premises unquestionably is that the two statements complete each other, or rather that the two acts are mutually supplementary, constituting together the performance of what had been before enjoined. As it is really one enumeration, therefore, it is *not* 'surprising' that the number given in both passages is 'identically the same.'

The silver yielded by the tribute was mainly used Ex. xxxviii. 27, for casting the 'sockets' or bases, on which the upright planks composing the frame of the tabernacle, and the pillars which supported the vail were to rest. These would be the last things needed before setting up the tabernacle. We are under no necessity, therefore, of assuming that the tribute was collected until near the first day of the first month in the second year of their departure out of Egypt, Ex. xl. 17. This month was largely taken up with the work of rearing the tabernacle, consecrating Aaron and his sons to the priesthood, setting the new ritual in operation and observing the annual passover. Then on the first day of the next month Num. i. 1, comes the order to 'take the sum of all the congregation.' In obedience to this, Moses and Aaron with their twelve assistants ver. 18, 'assembled all the congregation together on the first day of the second month, and they declared their pedigrees after their families, by the house of their fathers, according to the number of their names.' The simple meaning whereof we take to be, that they assembled the representatives of all the tribes, through whose agency the tribute had been already levied. They brought with them the tribute rolls, which it would be necessary to keep in order to certify that every one had paid. The names thus furnished were arranged according to their families and genealogies, and the entire number ascertained, which naturally enough corresponded with the number of half-shekels, which had been collected.

Colenso, however, fails to draw the inference which the facts, as he states them, so naturally warrant, not to say imperatively require. After telling us in language already quoted that in Ex. xxxviii. 26, "the *atonement-money* is collected; but nothing is there said of any *census* being taken," and in Num. i. 1–46, "the *census* is made, but there is no indication of any *atonement-money* being paid," he proceeds in the following remarkable manner.

"The omission in each case *might* be considered, of course, as accidental, (!) *it being supposed* that in the first instance the numbering really took place, and in the second the tribute was paid, *though neither circumstauce is mentioned.*"

And on this basis of what *might* be an *accident*, and this double *supposition* of what is *not mentioned*, Moses is convicted of saying something which his defamer regards as 'surprising.' If the Bishop had been so unmannerly as to charge not the Jewish legislator, but some living Englishman with uttering 'unhistorical' statements, would such a shew of evidence as this to substantiate it, save him from judgment of damages in a slander suit before any court of the realm?

But suppose we overlook these possible accidents and unmentioned suppositions, and concede to Colenso that both tribute and census were taken twice over with an interval of six months. And we shall not ask, what in the world Moses meant by taking a second census so soon. We know our author too well to imagine that he would be troubled by such a question. The gross absurdity would only be a fresh proof that the narrative is 'unhistorical.' But waiving all this, what is the result? "It is surprising that the number of adult males should have been identically the same" on both occasions.

We confess that if the fact were as Colenso alleges, it would not be so 'surprising' to us as it appears to be to him. It would be remarkable, certainly, but not incredible nor unaccountable. And in order to justify it to our mind, we would not be obliged to resort to the hypothesis, that through God's marvellous favour, no one had died in the six months, nor that the deaths had been to a man balanced by those who in the interval came of age, nor that the Levites were included in the first enumeration, though not in the second, and consequently the increase had been just equal to the number of that tribe; though it might puzzle him to disprove any one of these suppositions. But it is evident that we have only round numbers for the several tribes in Num. i. No units are given in any instance, but either fifties or even hundreds. Able expositors have hence been of the opinion that this tribute was not collected nor the enumeration made by assessing or reckoning every individual singly, but that the process was facilitated by basing it upon the decimal division of the host adopted some time before Ex. xviii. 25. The number of the people could be estimated, and the tribute raised from the rulers of thousands, of hundreds, of fifties or of tens with comparative readiness, and with sufficient accuracy. And if this were really the method adopted, it would leave a considerable margin for changes without these necessarily appearing in the enumeration. An army may have the same number of brigades, regiments, and companies, at the end of a campaign, that it had at the beginning. And if the changes in its ranks happened to be inconsiderable, an estimate in round numbers, where absolute accuracy is not insisted upon, would probably reveal no change at all.

CHAPTER VI.

THE ISRAELITES DWELLING IN TENTS.

THE mention of 'tents,' Ex. xvi. 16, sets the bishop to calculating again.

"Two millions of people would require 200,000 tents. How, then, did they acquire these?" "Further, if they had had these tents, how could they have carried them?" "This would require 500,000 oxen," even if the tents were "of the lightest modern material, whereas the Hebrew tents, *we must suppose*, were made of skins, and were, therefore, much heavier." "Thus they would have needed for this purpose 200,000 oxen."

This is really too childish to merit a serious reply. But if a person has undertaken to wade through a bog, he must not stop for mud; so we labour patiently on.

In the first place, then, the children of Israel were, as the narrative shows, very inadequately supplied with tents. It is not necessary to go beyond the pages of Colenso to demonstrate this sufficiently for our present purpose. We make the following extracts:

"In Lev. xxiii. 42, it is assigned as a reason for their 'dwelling in booths' for seven days at the feast of tabernacles, 'that your generations may know that I made the children of Israel to dwell in booths, when I brought them out of the land of Egypt.' It cannot be said that the word 'booths' here means 'tents;' because the Hebrew word for a *booth* made of boughs and bushes is quite different from that for a *tent*. And besides, in the context of the passage in Leviticus, we have a description of the way in which these booths were to be made. . . . This seems to fix the meaning of the Hebrew word in this particular passage, and to show that it is used in its proper sense of booths." Again, "we are told that on the first day, when they went out of Egypt, they 'journeyed from Rameses to Succoth,' Ex. xii. 37, where the name Succoth means *booths.*"

This, one would think, establishes clearly enough that large numbers of the people, and probably the vast majority of them, were destitute of tents, and were obliged to content themselves with such rude shelters as they could hastily construct from boughs of trees, bushes, or whatever came to hand. Such is not Colenso's inference, of course. "There is not," according to him, "the slightest indication in the story that they ever did live in booths." The mention of *booths* in these passages "conflicts strangely," in his judgment, with the allusion to *tents* in Ex. xvi. 16; but not so strangely, in our esteem, as his arguments and assertions do with the facts spread out upon his own pages.

Secondly, there are abundant means of explaining how the children of Israel became possessed of such tents as they had. We are required to believe," says the bishop, "that they had tents;" and then he springs at once to his conclusion that they had 200,000. If he will but be more moderate in his estimate, we shall try to relieve his anxiety as to the ways and means of procuring them.

1. The Israelites were largely engaged in tending flocks. This was their ancestral occupation, and the land of Goshen was assigned to them for the very purpose of allowing them to continue it under favourable circumstances and without offence to the Egyptians, Gen. xlvi. 32–34. Now, shepherds are in the Bible universally

spoken of as dwelling in tents from the days of Jabal and the patriarchs, Gen. iv. 20, xiii. 5. Comp. 1 Chron. iv. 39-41, v. 9, 10, 2 Chron. xiv. 15, Cant. i. 8, Isaiah xxxviii. 12, Jer. vi. 3, xlix. 29. The only exception is doubtful expression in Zeph. ii. 6, where, if our translators have hit the true sense, we read of '*cottages* for shepherds;' these, perhaps, may have been portable *booths* or sheds made of reeds, such as Diodorus* says were in use among Egyptian herdsmen down to his day. Ewald† thinks they were huts mounted on wagons, like those of the wandering Scythians.‡

2. The art of weaving was familiarly known in Egypt from the most ancient times. That the Israelites learned and practised it even in its finer and more elaborate applications, is apparent from the work of this description which they wrought for the tabernacle, Ex. xxxv. 25, and is further corroborated by 1 Chron. iv. 21. This would imply ability to make the coarse black hair-cloth which was used for tents in ancient, Cant. i. 5, as in modern times,§ even if this were not expressly stated, Ex. xxvi. 7, xxxv. 26, xxxvi. 14. In fact, we find mention of hair-cloth in the family of Jacob before the descent into Egypt, Gen. xxxvii. 34, comp. Rev. vi. 12, So that we do not see why "*we must suppose*" "the Hebrew tents were made of skins."

3. The Israelites had ample time to make every necessary preparation for their journey, while Pharaoh was

* Τὰς οἰκήσεις ἐκ τῶν καλάμων κατασκευάζεσθαι. Diodor. I. 43.

† Kleine Häuschen oder Karren der Hirten. Ewald, Propheten I. p. 367.

‡ Scythae,
Quorum plaustra vagas rite trahunt domos. Hor. Carm. III. 24, 10.

§ Robinson's Biblical Researches, I. p. 485; in the original edition, II. p. 180.

persisting in his refusal to let them go. But, says the Bishop, "had they provided this enormous number [of tents] in expectation of marching, when all their request was to be allowed to go 'for three days into the wilderness,' Ex. v. 3?"

Must we tell him that the chosen seed went down into Egypt only for a temporary sojourn, and that they were in constant expectation of being brought out of it to the land promised to their fathers? The exodus had been divinely foretold to Abraham, Gen. xv. 14. The assurance of it was repeated to Jacob, as he was on his way into Egypt, Gen. xlvi. 4. He testified his faith in it as he was dying (xlviii. 21), and directed that he should be buried in Canaan, xlix. 29. Joseph had the same confidence, and exacted an oath of his brethren that his bones should be carried up from Egypt when God visited his people, l. 24–26, Ex. xiii. 19. An explanation as old as the Targums (see Targ. on Cant. ii. 7) finds in 1 Chron. vii. 21 a premature attempt of the children of Ephraim to retake possession of Canaan. Moses, on his first arrival in Egypt, summoned the elders of the people and informed them that the time for their deliverance had come, Ex. iii. 16 etc., iv. 29 etc. How any sane man can believe after this that the Israelites had no further expectation than that of going 'for three days into the wilderness' is very 'surprising.' In order to exhibit Pharaoh's obduracy and unreasonableness no other request was made of him. But to infer from this, that nothing more was intended, is on a par with the reasoning which finds in God's command to Abraham to offer up his son an approval of human sacrifices.

4. The first allusion to tents occurs Ex. xvi. 1, a full month after their departure out of Egypt. This would

give additional time for their construction, and perhaps, also, for their purchase from the tribes of the desert.

And as to the mode of carrying these tents, together with their other baggage, will the Bishop please to inform us how he knows that they had not as many oxen as his most extravagant estimate supposes? Even on that hypothesis, one hundred men as rich as Job might have undertaken it on contract, Job xlii. 12. Colenso surely need not boggle at their having even 200,000, when he argues himself upon the supposition that they had "*two millions* of sheep and oxen," pp. 119, 122.

CHAPTER VII.

THE ISRAELITES ARMED.

HITHERTO remarks upon the Hebrew text have been only incidental and by the way: we now come upon a chapter which is, *ex professo*, devoted to this subject. The former have proved so refreshing that we may well anticipate a choice display of learning and criticism. The passage to which we are indebted for so rare an entertainment is

Ex. xiii. 18. The children of Israel went up *harnessed* (חֲמֻשִׁים) out of the land of Egypt.

The word here rendered 'harnessed,' is one of the few to be met with in the Hebrew Bible whose meaning and derivation are exceedingly doubtful, and which has accordingly been variously translated, from the old Greek interpreters downward. In such cases lexicographers have heretofore been under the delusion that one essential condition of a true rendering is that it must suit every passage in which the word occurs; or, if this is impossible, different senses must be assumed, sufficient to meet the exigencies of every case. The labours of Colenso mark the opening of a new era. The meanings of difficult words are henceforth to be determined so that they will *not* suit the context in which they stand. It is scarcely possible to overestimate the results which might flow from the ingenious and persevering application of this hitherto undiscovered principle. Those critics, especially, who are interested in proving the statements of an author 'unhistorical,' will find the invention particularly valuable.

That we are not exalting the merits of this invention unduly we can satisfy our readers, by exhibiting its operation in the present instance. We are first told that the word חֲמֻשִׁים *appears* to mean 'armed,' or 'in battle array.' Inasmuch as these two meanings are far from being coincident, we might ask which is to be preferred? and why? Does it mean that the people were drawn up in regular ranks, or that they had arms in their hands? Without pausing, however, over such impertinent questions, without even intimating that he is restricting the signification of the word beyond his own statement of it, our author proceeds on the assumption that it means 'armed,' and that *only*, adding immediately, "it is inconceivable, however, that these down-trodden, oppressed people should have been allowed by Pharaoh to possess arms." One would suppose from this that he was about correcting an opinion too hastily formed, and modifying a definition which he finds not to meet the exigencies of the case. But no! the inappropriate meaning is left undisturbed. It does not prove Colenso wrong, but the narrative false.

Gesenius defines the word (see his Lexicon translated by Prof. Robinson) *fierce*, *active*, *eager*, *brave* in battle. Would it not have been well to have stated his reasons, if he had any, for setting this definition aside? At least would it not have been candid to have mentioned the fact, which is strangely omitted in his disquisition, that the standard lexicographer of the day had assigned these meanings to it? What has he to object to the representation that the children of Israel went out of the land of their bondage like a victorious army, laden with spoils and with all the *eager impetuosity*, which characterizes such a host?

In order to prove that the Israelites could not have had arms in their possession, he makes the following most unlucky allusion to the father of history.

"The warriors formed a distinct caste in Egypt, as Herodotus tells us, ii. 165, 'being in number, when they are most numerous, 160,000, none of whom learn any mechanical art, but apply themselves wholly to military affairs.'"

The unaccountable negligence of this quotation, to call it nothing worse, will appear in the first place from the fact, that Herodotus is there speaking of but one division of the "caste" of native warriors. In the very next paragraph he speaks of another division amounting to 250,000. In the second place, these native warriors did not exclude mercenaries, as he would have seen if he had read the second paragraph before the one from which he quotes; not to say that he might have learned it from the prophet Jeremiah xlvi. 21. Rawlinson in his Herodotus, vol. ii. p. 199, remarks that "the ancient kings in the glorious times of Egypt's great power had foreign auxiliaries; they were levies composing part of the army, like those of the various nations which contributed to the expeditions of Xerxes and other Persian monarchs." Wilkinson in his Manners and Customs of the Ancient Egyptians, vol. i. p. 287, says, "Besides the native corps they had also mercenary troops, who were enrolled either from the nations in alliance with the Egyptians, or from those who had been conquered by them . . . . Strabo speaks of them as mercenaries; and the *million of men* he mentions must have included these foreign auxiliaries." Can Colenso prove that Pharaoh did not make use of Israelites in his army as Great Britain does of Sepoys in India? And besides, in spite of his sneer at the idea of 'borrowing' arms, can he prove that the Egyptians did not supply the Israelites with these as well as other necessaries for their journey, in their urgency to have them go?

As the Bishop has been studying this subject "less than two years" (p. 12), he cannot be expected as yet to have read very extensively upon it. We would advise him, however, not to meddle much with Egyptian antiquities. The less that is said about them by one who undertakes to prove the Pentateuch 'unhistorical,' the better. These antiquities furnish too many evidences both of its truth and of its having been written in the midst of the scenes which it describes.

Apart, however, from "the stubborn word חֲמֻשִׁים," the bishop tells us "*we must suppose* that the whole body of 600,000 warriors were armed, when they were numbered, Num. i. 3." Why so? If he had ever heard of the American militia system before the war which now desolates this continent, he would have known that to be enrolled as 'able to go forth to war,' and to be armed, are not convertible expressions. "And, besides, where did they get the armour with which about a month after [leaving Egypt] they fought the Amalekites, Ex. xvii. 8–13?" We presume that a battle might be fought without the entire 600,000 being armed and engaging in it.

But if "they had come to be possessed of arms, is it conceivable that 600,000 armed men, in the prime of life, would have cried out in panic terror 'sore afraid,'

Ex. xiv. 10, when they saw that they were being pursued?" We hope that by this time the ingenuity of the Bishop's device, and the marvellous success of his invention will be apparent. The method, it will be seen, need not be confined to strict lexicography. The range of its applicability equals that of the philosopher's stone. It can be applied to anything whatever, and invariably with the same result. Fix your theory so that it shall *not* correspond with the facts, and then woe be to the facts! Arrive at your conclusion from an *ex parte* statement of the case; after this has been settled, introduce the considerations which are incompatible with it, and the falsity of the narrative follows of course. It would be in vain to expect the Bishop to reconsider his argument on account of this or any other difficulty, that may be in the way. That is Moses' concern, not his. All that remains for us, is timidly to suggest that the unexpected appearance of Pharaoh's chariots might spread terror in an undisciplined throng, encumbered as the Israelites were, even if they had arms in their hands, as one of the formidable iron-clads of modern times might drive any number of infantry beyond the reach of its death-dealing guns. Comp. Judg. iv. 3.

The philological argument of this chapter, then, amounts to this. The word חֲמֻשִׁים means either *armed* or *in battle array* (though Gesenius defines it differently); therefore the Israelites *had arms;* therefore they were *all armed.* But they could not have been all armed. Therefore the narrative is untrue. The question involuntarily forces itself upon us, Is not a residence among the Zulus unfavourable to the development of the understanding?

The remarks and calculations, with which we are further favoured, respecting the alternate hypothesis that the word חֲמֻשִׁים is radically connected with the numeral *five*, and that it consequently means "five in a rank," present abundant matter for comment. As they are of no consequence to the argument, however, we pass them by, simply observing that, upon like principles, a garrison *decimated* by disease must have lost precisely one-tenth, and winter-*quarters* must mean the fourth part of something.

How if the word has the sense, which Cocceius attributes to it, of *numbered* or *belonging to a numbered host?* It would then be equivalent to the Greek πεμπάζω, which denotes strictly (see Liddell and Scott) *to count on five fingers*, or *count by fives*, then generally *to count.* And the Latin *numeri* is used as a military term for *a division of an army.* Or how, if חֲמֻשִׁים means, what Gesenius says it would, if it were referred to the numeral *five*, *quinquepartitum*, or consisting of five parts, the centre, the two wings, and the front and rear guard, and hence obtains the more general sense *in battle array?* What would then become of his calculation that "they must have formed a column sixty-eight miles long, and it would have taken several days to have *started* them all off, instead of their going out all together that self-same day?"

CHAPTER VIII.

THE INSTITUTION OF THE PASSOVER.

THE next chapter, headed as above, is so transparent and glaring a misrepresentation, that no one can be deceived by it, and we cannot persuade ourselves to delay upon it. The whole seeming force of it rests upon the assumption and the assertion, directly in the face of the plain statements of the narrative, that the first instructions to the children of Israel respecting the passover were given to them on the day that it was to be killed, and that the 'borrowing' from the Egyptians was done "at a moment's notice."

It is true that they were directed, Ex. xii. 3, to take the lamb on the tenth day of the month, and, ver. 6, to keep it up until the fourteenth, and then kill it. But this, instead of showing that they had at least four days' notice, only makes "the story" "perplexing and contradictory!" For does not the LORD say, in the very same connection, ver. 12, 'I will pass through the land of Egypt *this* night'? This is further fortified by an appeal to the original Hebrew; "the expression is distinctly הַזֶּה, *this*, not הַהוּא, *that*." We fear that the Bishop and his Hebrew dictionary are comparative strangers to each other; how else could he have overlooked the fact, that one of the meanings of זֶה is *that which has just been men-*

tioned (Gesen. *sub verbo*), a sense in which it is frequently rendered 'the same' in the common English version, e. g. Gen. vii. 11, 13, Ex. xix. 1. 'This night,' according to Hebrew usage, means the night spoken of immediately before, and not necessarily the one succeeding the moment of speaking. If Colenso continues his investigations, we expect to hear of a much more serious difficulty than this in Deut. ix. 1. Moses there says to Israel, 'Thou art to pass over Jordan *this day*.' We must accordingly assume that all that follows to the end of the book, including the death of Moses and the thirty days mourning for him, took place within the next twelve hours.

The allegation that the 'borrowing' was performed "at a moment's notice," is, if possible, yet more inexcusable. The people were not only told what to do, at least four days beforehand, Ex. xi. 2, but they were spoken to on the subject when Moses first returned to Egypt, Ex. iii. 21, 22, iv. 30.

The "second notice, to start," given "at midnight," is a fabrication of Colenso's own. The people had been instructed how to act long before; and the urgency of the Egyptians to send them out of the country, Ex. xii. 33, left them no option.

All the computations of the chapter about sheep, and territory, and population, and the time required to circulate notices, however interesting in themselves, are nothing to the purpose, for which they are alleged, of proving the statements of Moses self-contradictory or incredible. There is a Hebrew criticism embedded in this discussion, however, which, whether just or not, is of so striking a nature, that it would be unpardonable not to mention it. Jehovah was to "*stride across* (פסח)

the threshold, and protect the house from the angel of death." 'Passover,' then, is a misnomer; the festival should be called *Stride-over.* We commend this to the careful consideration of the children of Abraham.

CHAPTER IX.

THE MARCH OUT OF EGYPT.

UNDER this caption we are first presented with a re-hash of the unfounded assumptions of the preceding chapter respecting the suddenness of the call to leave Egypt. Then follow a few more of the same sort. After being summoned "suddenly at midnight," the "two millions" of Israelites "come in from all parts of the land of Goshen to Rameses," and were then "started again from Rameses that very same day, and marched on to Succoth." Finally, "on the third day, they turned aside and 'encamped by the sea.' Ex. xiv. 2."

In proof that they came in from Goshen to Rameses just, as it would seem, for the sake of marching back again, he appeals to Ex. xii. 37—'And the children of Israel journeyed from Rameses to Succoth, about six hundred thousand on foot that were men, beside children.'

The following view of the case which Colenso himself quotes from Kurtz, is intrinsically so probable, that it must commend itself, we think, to every sober-minded person, and show both the needlessness and inadmissibility of the preceding hypothesis. Kurtz says, "Rameses was the capital of the province. There, no doubt, Moses and Aaron were residing. The procession started thence;

and after the main body had set out, smaller parties came from all directions, as speedily as possible, and joined it at the point of the road nearest to their own dwellings."

Suppose, however, that we allow all the marching and countermarching which the Bishop wishes to foist into the narrative, how would this affect the credit of the sacred historian? The objector wishes us to believe that the time into which this was crowded was too limited for its performance. After reaching Rameses they were fifty or sixty miles from the sea, and this could not be traversed by such an immense host against 'the third day.'

But this 'third day' is a pure figment; there is nothing said about it in Exodus. Moses does not tell us how long it took the people to reach the Red Sea. He mentions indeed that they went "from Rameses to Succoth, from Succoth to Etham, and from Etham to the Red Sea." But it is nowhere stated that they were only a day in passing from one of these points to that next in order. And that this is not his meaning appears from the fact that if their marches after crossing the Red Sea, Ex. xv. 22–xvi. 1, be interpreted in the same way, they ought to have reached the wilderness of Sin in ten days, whereas a month was consumed in getting there.

And here the Bishop is guilty of downright dishonesty in garbling a quotation from Kurtz to suit his purposes. Professing to give the views of that eminent scholar, he carefully conceals from his readers the opinion which Kurtz strenuously maintains and in our judgment incontrovertibly establishes, that the distance from one station or place of encampment to another may as naturally be several days' journey as one, compare Num. xxxiii. 8. This is kept back not only by omitting what Kurtz says on that point, but by sundering the quotations, which are made, from their true connection so as to produce a false impression of their meaning, by transposing a sentence for the same purpose, and more fraudulently still, by omitting the following sentence from what purports to be a connected quotation, viz. "The following considerations also serve to show, that the Israelites must necessarily have spent *more than three days* on their march from Rameses to their encampment by the sea." This suggestion would be fatal to all his quibbling objections. And as there was no reply that could be made to it, he chose an easy but dishonourable method of ridding himself of all perplexity. What would the "simple-minded but intelligent" Zulus say to such conduct as this on the part of their bishop? If he has, as he claims (p. 35), "renounced the hidden things of dishonesty" it must be in a sense widely different from that in which the apostle intended the phrase.

The question raised at the close of this chapter as to the subsistence of the people and their flocks upon the march properly belongs to the chapter next ensuing.

CHAPTER X.

THE SHEEP AND CATTLE OF THE ISRAELITES IN THE DESERT.

"The people, we are told, were supplied with manna. But there was no miraculous provision of food for the herds and flocks." How, then, did the latter gather subsistence in that inhospitable wilderness?

It is so obvious that the vast multitude of men and animals, which went out of Egypt with Moses, could not have been supported in the desert for forty years by mere natural means, that this has always been a great stumbling-block to those who insist upon measuring the facts of the Bible by the standard of ordinary history. But if any think to escape this difficulty by denying the truth of the facts, they will only involve themselves in others which are still more insurmountable.

All Jewish history is a fable, if the Exodus be untrue. Not to insist upon the corroborations from profane historians, which would thus be unaccounted for, the Egyptian Manetho, Tacitus, Justin, and others, everything in Judaism is built upon it, and presupposes it. How did such a tradition originate, or ever gain prevalence, if it were false? There was nothing in it to gratify national vanity, but everything to humiliate it, and to shock their prejudices. That their fathers had been in bondage to the uncircumcised Egyptians,—that they had grown to be a nation, not on the sacred soil of Palestine, but in the profane land of idolaters—that the most solemn revelations of Jehovah, including the fundamental law of their nation, were given not at Jerusalem, but in a desert two hundred miles away,—that a whole generation of their fathers had been so faithless as to be doomed to die in the desert, and even the great lawgiver himself, and the first high priest had been debarred from entering the holy land; is it conceivable that these were inventions of the Jewish mind, or that they ever could have entered into the faith of the nation if they were not undeniable facts?

Moreover, these are not vague uncertain traditions, which were spoken of doubtfully, or stated variously at different times and places, though even if this were the case we would still be obliged to assume a historical *basis* to account satisfactorily for their origin. But in all that multitude of allusions to the subject or declarations respecting it, which abound throughout the Old Testament, there is no hesitation and no diversity. The same story is told, or is implied everywhere. There can be no question that it expresses the universal faith of the Israelitish people.

But further, when did this story originate and under what circumstances? We have in the first place, in the Pentateuch, a contemporaneous history of the march from Egypt to Canaan. For though Colenso may scoff and deride its claims, these are too firmly established to be shaken. But besides this, we can trace it through the entire subsequent literature of the Hebrews from first to last. Prophets, psalmists, historians, speak of it as well known and undeniable. The book of Joshua belonging to the age next succeeding that of Moses, and written by one who participated in the miraculous crossing of the Jordan, Josh. v. 1, lends it the most unequivocal sanction and is in fact inexplicable on every page without it. Or if Colenso could succeed in sweeping away both Joshua and the Pentateuch by the potent wand of his arithmetical criticism, Judges would utter its testimony, ii. 1, *et passim.* Even unbelieving critics do not venture to deny the antiquity and originality of the song of Deborah, and that makes express mention of the supernatural revelation at Sinai, Judg. v. 5, which implies and sanctions all the rest.

But there is more to be explained than the existence of written testimonies of too early a date and too near the time of the event, to admit of the growth of an unfounded tradition, even if such a tradition could have originated in the Jewish mind after any lapse of time, or if such uniformity of statement on the part of such a multitude of voices could be accounted for otherwise than by the supposition of the truth of what is thus attested. The facts of Jewish history presuppose what the Pentateuch records, and are susceptible of no other solution. The fragments of aboriginal tribes occupying portions of Canaan along with Israel, some of them, as the Philistines, even long disputing the prëeminence with them, show that Israel had intruded themselves from abroad and thrust out the primitive possessors of the soil. The peculiar position of the tribe of Levi, dispersed among the other tribes, and owning no inheritance of its own, implies its separation to sacerdotal service before Canaan had been entered. That the sanctuary of God was a tent or tabernacle prior to the erection of Solomon's temple implies the migratory sojourn in the wilderness.

And not only facts like these, which cannot be denied or explained away, if all history is not to be dissolved into a mere illusion, but the permanent institutions of Israel bear the ineffaceable impress of the exodus. The annual passover and the feast of tabernacles were public stated commemorations of the coming out of Egypt and the abode in the wilderness. These were instituted at the time when the events themselves took place, and were perpetuated ever since, fathers to sons explaining the meaning of the observance. The pot of manna and Aaron's rod that budded were preserved in the sanctuary, and the brazen serpent was in existence until the days of Hezekiah, 2 Kings xviii. 4. And then, there is the ceremonial, which, with all its multitudinous prescriptions, has nevertheless such a unity of purpose and of idea, as shows that it is no conglomerate made up of the slow accretions of ages, and of heterogeneous materials gathered from diverse quarters, but is a consistent system, the work of one mind, and introduced in its completeness. Now, this points to the wilderness as the place of its origin, by numerous injunctions, which enter as constituent parts into the ceremonial system, and yet which derive their form from the circumstances of that period, e. g. the minute specifications respecting the transportation of the tabernacle and its furniture, Num. iv. 5 etc., the burning of parts of certain sacrifices without the *camp*, Lev. iv. 12, the removal of lepers without the *camp*, Lev. xiii. 46. And still further, the ceremonial contains not a few undoubted Egyptian elements. These are not so numerous nor so pervading as Spencer maintained in the interest of rationalism, and yet they are sufficient to show beyond question that the people must have stood in an intimate relation to

Egypt at the time when this system was given to them.

This is no prejudice to the inspiration of Moses, or to the divinity of the law given through him. It neither disproves nor degrades the inspiration of the apostles that they taught heavenly truths to the world in the language of Greece. Nor are the sublime revelations of Ezekiel and of Daniel less truly from God, because clothed in the garb of symbols suggested or modified by the colossal and grotesque forms perpetually before their eyes in Babylonia. With the symbolical language of Egypt both Moses and the people were familiar. The religion of Egypt, with its absurd abominations, the lawgiver utterly discards. But in setting forth the pure and heavenly truths of the religion of the true God, he draws upon symbols with which they were already acquainted, purging them from every heathenish and false association, and bringing them into such connections that they aptly represent precisely what he would have them teach. It is just as the apostles adopted words which in the mouths of pagan Greeks had low and unworthy senses, and infused into them the spirit of the Christian revelation, thus regenerating the language while they used it. And as the idiom of the New Testament affords an index to the time, the country, and the circumstances in which it was written, so the idiom of the ceremonial of Moses, if we may so speak, the character and affinities of the symbols which he employs, show it to have come from a man familiar with Egyptian institutions, and to have been introduced into Israel at a period when the people possessed such a familiarity likewise.

These considerations thus hastily hinted at, and which

might be corroborated and expanded indefinitely, show beyond a doubt that the great facts of the exodus are true. Colenso may cavil and calculate till doomsday, but he cannot unsettle what is thus woven into the very texture of everything relating to the Israelitish people, their history, their literature, and their institutions. Here are indisputable facts to be accounted for, which no imposture could have effected and which no mystification can obscure. We affirm unhesitatingly that no hypothesis can be framed which will satisfactorily account for them, but that of the truth of the narrative, marvellous as it may be, which is given by Moses. And hence, as Colenso acknowledges, even a man like Ewald, proverbial in Germany itself for stopping at no extravagance of criticism and no wildness of hypothesis, feels compelled to confess, if the whole history of Israel is not to be frittered away, that the fact of the exodus and of the sojourn in the wilderness is undeniably true.

"Ewald certainly asserts this," viz. that "the general truth of the wanderings in the wilderness is an essential preliminary to the whole of the subsequent history of Israel;" "but I cannot find any place where he *shows* it. The story of the Exodus is no doubt an 'essential preliminary' to *certain parts* of the subsequent history of Israel, as recorded, but not to the whole of it. If that story be shown to be untrue, those parts may also have to be abandoned as untrue, but not the whole Jewish history."

We would like to have the Bishop specify which these 'certain parts' of the history are that he would be willing to give up for the sake of getting rid of the Exodus. We fancy there would be very little left. He might as well undertake to explain American history on the hypothesis that this country was not settled from Europe.

The fact must be accepted, therefore, with all its difficulties. This vast multitude of men and animals did march into the desert, and continued there for forty years. How did they subsist?

We reply, in the first place, that the natural productions of the region, in which they were, would go a certain length toward their support. This feature of the case has not always received its due share of attention. The miracle, which must be admitted in any event, is so stupendous and long-continued, that it seems to be scarcely enhanced to an appreciable extent by leaving all ordinary supplies out of the account. And, further, the inspired historian very properly exalts the miraculous side of the case, which was so out of proportion to what was merely natural, and which was the aspect with which he was chiefly concerned, to special and almost exclusive prominence. Not that he exaggerates the miracle, or studiously conceals the other available means of subsistence; but he lays no stress upon the latter. And hence the hints and indications which he does give upon the subject have so frequently—perhaps we might say commonly—been overlooked; e. g. the mention of date palms, Ex. xv. 27, the nourishment obtained from the flocks which they are said to have had with them, and the purchase of food and drink for themselves and their cattle, Num. xx. 19, Deut. ii. 6, 28.

The tendency of late, among students of this portion of the sacred record, has, however, been toward the opposite extreme of under-estimating the miracle and exalting unduly the natural resources of the region. And this for a triple reason; first, the general tendency in one extreme of opinion to generate its opposite; secondly, the interest of unbelief, which, unable to rid itself of the fact of the exodus, sought to explain it upon a natural basis; and thirdly, the pardonable enthusiasm of those who, in their recent explorations of this region, have added so much to our knowledge of its character, and brought to light so much that was unexpected, that it is not surprising if they attribute a greater weight to their discoveries than a cooler judgment will be disposed to allow. If, therefore, we wish to arrive at a correct impression of the real state of the case, we must carefully avoid both extremes, and diligently examine whatever sources of information lie within our reach.

Now, the fact is, that while the general features of the Sinaitic desert are, as described in the long pages of citations made by Colenso, those of aridity, barrenness, and desolation, there are, nevertheless, exceptions to this in verdant oases and fertile wadys scattered here and there.*

* We clip from the pages of Colenso the following quotations to show the possibilities of culture in this desert. The first is taken from Stanley's Sinai and Palestine, p. 27 of the American edition:

" 'How much may be done by a careful use of such water and such soil as the desert supplies, may be seen by the only two spots, to which, now, a diligent and provident attention is paid, namely, the gardens at the Wells of Moses, under the care of the French and English agents from Suez, and the gardens in the valleys of Jebel Musa, under the care of the Greek monks of the convent of St. Catherine. Even so late as the seventeenth century, if we may trust the expression of MONCONYS, the Wady-er-Rahah, in front of the convent, now entirely bare, was "a vast green plain," *une grande champagne verte.*' "

The quotation marks in the printed copy of Colenso are here incorrect. Stanley himself quotes the words "a vast green plain."

The second is from Shaw, Travels to the Holy Land, ch. ii. :—

" 'Though nothing that can properly be called soil is to be found in these parts of Arabia, these monks have, in a long process of time, covered over with dung and the sweepings of their convent near four acres of these naked rocks, which produce as good cabbages, salads, roots, and all kinds of pot-herbs, as any soil and climate whatsoever. They have likewise

These suffice to sustain a sparse population at the present day. The roving tribes which frequent the desert are very inconsiderable, it is true, as compared with the immense host of the Israelites; still they show that the region is not absolutely destitute of vegetation. Ritter,* (p. 709,) after describing the district in the immediate vicinity of Sinai, adds:

"We adduce these data here just to confirm anew, what has been so often proved already, that it is only our ignorance which creates such great deserts, such unpeopled solitudes, such void spaces in the earth; these are constantly vanishing more and more from the Sahara and the so-called absolute deserts of Arabia and Petrea, as they have done from the midst of the primeval forests of America (see Stevens, Catherwood, etc.), with every serious advance of investigation into these regions."

But further, there are abundant indications that this desert once supported a much larger population than at present, just as the same is the case with Palestine itself; and the causes of this increased sterility in modern times can, in a measure, be pointed out. On this subject, we may be indulged with a somewhat extended quotation from Ritter, pp. 926, 927, the great authority on all questions of physical geography.

"We have already, above, referred to the former natural condition of things in this country, and their relations, which must have been essentially different in their effects from those of the present. So the former

---

raised apple, pear, plum, almond, and olive trees, not only in great numbers, but also of excellent kinds. Their grasses also are not inferior, either in size or flavour, to any whatsoever. Thus this little garden demonstrates how far an indefatigable industry may prevail over nature.'"

Now whatever the Bishop may choose to say about "little gardens," "a few favoured spots," "great care and industry," and "a long process of time," such facts as the above show that the desolation is not absolute, nor is it universally irredeemable.

* This and the following reference to Ritter have respect to Theil xiv. of his Erdkunde, which treats of the Peninsula of Sinai.

abundance of vegetation,* especially in the larger and more numerous growth of trees, with the vanishing of which the number of smaller plants must diminish likewise. So the greater abundance of various articles of food, of which the people of Israel in their time might make use. So the more universal and thorough cultivation of the soil, which reveals itself in the monumental periods of the most ancient Egyptians, their mining operations and settlements, as well as in the Christian period by episcopal foundations and the remains, which are scattered everywhere, of cloisters, hermitages, walls, gardens, fields, and wells. So also, finally, in the possibility of a better improvement of the temporary abundance of water in the wadys as well as of the rain, showers of which are not uncommon, but which could only be preserved by industry and artificial means for more unfruitful seasons of the year, as this is the case in other districts under the same parallel of latitude.

"These relations, taken together and supported by the numerous inscriptions on Sinai and Serbal, along with those in Wady Mokatteb and in a hundred other ravines, and those on the tops of rocks and mountains, which are at present found in wild solitude and perfect neglect, inscribed by human hands in all directions through the entire central group of mountains, show that more numerous populations could subsist here, and actually did subsist, even if we did not likewise know that before the passage of Israel, four different nationalities, the sons of Amalek, Midian, and Ishmael, and on the east the Edomites, had their seats here, and maintained them, whose number we could not estimate to be trifling, even if we were to reduce them to a minimum, and make them to have been of the smallest dimensions of modern Arab tribes.

"We agree, therefore, perfectly with the critical historian Ewald, when he says, that this peninsula could support far more people then than at present —amidst great destitutions, to be sure, which are frequently spoken of in the reminiscences of the people, and which also served a purpose in trying them; but yet so that their existence need not have been endangered thereby. From the trifling number of its present negligent population, no conclusion surely can be drawn with certainty as to its former condition, any more than this can be done in the case of many other regions of the world—*e. g.* Sogdiana, etc.—which were once in a glorious state of cultivation, but which are now, in like manner, desolated by human indolence."

---

* Under this and each of the particulars which follow, Ritter refers back to detailed descriptions previously given in his work, confirming and elucidating the summary statement here made.

Colenso repeats Stanley's allusion in his Sinai and Palestine to this very passage of Ritter, as containing a good summing up of the indications that the mountains of Sinai were once "able to furnish greater resources than at present." And without giving himself the trouble to look up the passage, as it would appear, he dismisses it in the following characteristic and flippant manner. "Whatever they may be, they cannot do away with the plain language of the Bible already quoted, which shows that the general character of the desert was as desolate and barren then as now." While paying all due respect to such an unwonted instance of reverence for "the plain language of the Bible," as to adhere to it unshrinkingly, without caring even to listen to what modern investigation can adduce, we venture to doubt whether its meaning is as he alleges.

The following are the passages, with the comments, italics, and all, which are relied upon to prove that the country traversed by the Israelites has undergone no

"material change from that time to this. It is described as being then what it is now, a 'desert land,' a 'waste howling wilderness,' Deut. xxxii. 10. 'Why have ye brought up the congregation of the LORD into this wilderness, that we and our cattle should die there? And wherefore have ye made us to come up out of Egypt, to bring us in unto this evil place? It is no place of seed, or of figs, or of vines, or of pomegranates; *neither is there any water to drink.*' Num. xx. 4, 5. From this passage it appears also that the water from the rock did *not* follow them, as some have supposed. 'Beware that thou forget not the LORD thy God . . . . who led thee through that great and terrible wilderness, wherein were fiery serpents, and scorpions, and drought, *where there was no water*,' Deut. viii. 15. 'Neither said they, Where is the LORD that brought us up out of the land of Egypt, that led us through the wilderness, through a land of deserts and of pits, through a land of drought and of the shadow of death, through a land that no man passed through, and where no man dwelt?' Jer. ii. 6."

All this proves that the region was a desert then.

And it is a desert now. But of its comparative sterility then and now, the text says nothing. No accumulation of epithets could express too strongly how utterly incapable such a region was without miraculous interference of affording the needed supplies for so vast a multitude during so many years. But so far from establishing an absolute destitution of all vegetation, the expressions employed above prove rather the reverse. The original word for 'wilderness' מִדְבָּר, means properly *pasture-land*, a tract of country, which is unfit for cultivation, but where cattle are driven; this Colenso appears to have forgotten here, though he remembers it on p. 189, where he has an object to serve by it. 'Howling' implies the presence of wild beasts, which of course must find something to live upon. And it is obvious that the language of the prophet, 'a land that no man passed through, and where no man dwelt,' is simply intended as a strong description of the dreary and inhospitable nature of the region, and not as a categorical assertion that not a single individual had ever passed through it, or dwelt in it, as Colenso seems to understand it. Because the narrative of Moses makes it sufficiently plain that other persons had been in it before, and were in it then.

Now as to the subsistence of the cattle, from which the Bishop draws his chief objection, what is to prevent their feeding in the various wadys of the peninsula? That pasturage was to be found in the vicinity of Sinai is expressly declared Ex. xxxiv. 3, and is implied in Moses leading his father-in-law's flocks to that very place, Ex. iii. 1. Winer, whom none can charge with attaching undue weight to the authority of Scripture, says* with

* Biblisches Realwörterbuch, vol. II. p. 708. Art. *Wüste Arabische.*

an eye to the evidences already reviewed of a higher measure of fertility in this region in former times than at present: "The flocks enjoying a change of pasture could not easily suffer for want of food."

But Colenso is not willing to allow them this change of pasture.

"It cannot be supposed, as some have suggested, that the flocks and herds were scattered far and wide, during the sojourn of the people in the wilderness, and so were able the more easily to find pasture. The story says nothing, and implies nothing, whatever of this; but, as far as it proves anything, it proves the contrary, since we find the whole body of the people together, on all occasions specified in the history. If, indeed, they had been so dispersed, they would surely have required to be guarded, by large bodies of armed men, from the attacks of the Amalekites, Midianites, and others.

"It seems to be clearly implied in Num. ix. 17–23 that they travelled all together, and were not separated into different bodies."

This is sheer trifling. Moses does not profess to give any account of the manner in which the cattle were driven. It might be supposed that the cattle of the patriarchs were always in the vicinity of their residence, and yet we incidentally learn upon one occasion that Jacob's flocks were feeding sixty miles from home, Gen. xxxvii. 17.

We have no idea, however, that the subsistence of Israel's flocks in the wilderness is wholly explicable from natural causes, any more than we have that the subsistence of the people themselves can be so explained. It is true that nothing is expressly said of a miraculous provision being made for the flocks as was made for the people by the gift of manna. But we do not accept the dictum that no miracles are to be assumed but such as are expressly mentioned in the sacred history. Our Saviour's public ministry abounded in miracles, so that the evangelist tells us that the world itself could not contain the books which would have to be written to describe them all, John xxi. 25. And yet only a few of these mighty works were narrated by way of specimen.

It was so doubtless at the time of the exodus. A few characteristic specimens only are related, while numbers are left untold. The whole period was one of supernatural guidance, protection, and supply, Deut. xxxii. 10. Divine interference to whatever extent the necessities of Israel's position demanded was the rule, not the exception. The idea that God would provide by miracle for the wants of Israel, even preserve their shoes and clothes from waxing old, Deut. xxix. 5, and yet fail to supply their cattle with what was absolutely necessary for their support, is like Colenso's idea that if God arrested the earth's rotation at the prayer of Joshua, "every human being and animal would be dashed to pieces in a moment, and a mighty deluge overwhelm the earth." (p. 9.)

The fact that it is not in so many terms declared that a miracle was wrought, is no evidence against it, if statements are made and facts recorded, which necessarily imply a miracle. In the narrative of raising Jairus' daughter, it is simply said, Mat. ix. 25, that Jesus 'went in and took her by the hand and the maid arose.' The evangelist does not say that it was a miracle. He simply records the fact that the dead was recovered by a touch, and suffers his readers to draw their own inferences. When it is said that Moses passed forty days and forty nights without eating or drinking, Ex. xxxiv. 28, and the same thing is likewise recorded of Elijah, 1 Kin. xix. 8, and of our Lord, Mat. iv. 2, must we look to the ordinary laws of physiology for an explanation, because the fact is not expressly declared to have been miraculous?

The sacred history records that Israel took an immense number of flocks and herds into the wilderness, that they were sustained there and brought safely out again. Now the more successful Colenso is in establishing that this vast multitude of animals could not have found subsistence by natural means, the more clearly he proves that there must have been some divine interposition in the case. In what form this interposition was manifested we cannot tell. All we know is that the events recorded did take place; and if they could not have occurred without a miracle, then there must have been a miracle. It may have been in the same way that the widow's handful of meal was made to sustain her family and Elijah, till God sent rain upon the earth, and as the five loaves and two fishes were made to feed five thousand men. Or it may have been by converting the wilderness into a fruitful field, and a dry land into springs of water.

The Psalmist says, cvii. 35–38, 'He turneth the wilderness into a standing water, and dry ground into water-springs; and there he maketh the hungry to dwell that they may prepare a city for habitation, and sow the fields and plant vineyards, which may yield fruits of increase. He blesseth them also, so that they are multiplied greatly; and *suffereth not their cattle to decrease.*' Like expressions occur also in the prophets, Isa. xxxii. 15, xxxv. 7, xli. 18. In the frequency with which the sacred writers draw upon the past to image forth the future, is it not more than probable that in using such language, they had before their minds the great historical example of what they are depicting in Israel's march through the desert? There is nothing here certainly in any view of the subject to trouble any man who is able to do, what the Bishop says he can, "believe and receive the miracles of Scripture heartily, if only they are authenticated by a veracious history," p. 51. And even those who can persuade themselves that the plagues of Egypt and the passage of the Red Sea were simply wonderful conjunctures of extraordinary natural phenomena need have little difficulty, one would think, in extending these natural marvels a little further, and conceiving of rain and grass abounding in the desert at just that time, as it has never done before or since.

The Bishop has one more question to raise, which, he says, "is not generally taken into consideration at all." In fact we are not sure that it is not original with himself. "They must have passed the whole of the winter months under Sinai and must have found it bitterly cold." Where then did they find fuel? We do not know that we can do better than to refer him for information to the hewers of wood, and drawers of water, spoken of in Deut. xxix. 11. Perhaps it was where they found the timbers for the tabernacle, Ex. xxvi. 15; perhaps it was where the man went to gather sticks upon the Sabbath-day, Num. xv. 32; perhaps the wood from which the modern Arabs make their charcoal for the Egyptian markets (p. 127), may be a remnant of what the Israelites discovered and appropriated.

CHAPTER XI.

THE NUMBER OF THE ISRAELITES COMPARED WITH THE EXTENT OF THE LAND OF CANAAN.

THE difficulty alleged in this chapter is the following:

"The whole land, which was divided among the tribes in the time of Joshua, including the countries beyond the Jordan, was in extent about 11,000 square miles, or 7,000,000 acres. And, according to the story, this was occupied by more than two millions of people."

How, then, could God have spoken to Israel as he is said to have done in Ex. xxiii. 29, 30? 'I will not drive them [viz. the former occupants of the country] out from before thee in one year, lest the land become desolate, and the beast of the field multiply against thee. By little and little I will drive them out from before thee, until thou be increased and inherit the land.' To make the absurdity of this apparent, a statement is given from the census of 1851 of the number of acres and the amount of population in "the three English agricultural counties of Norfolk, Suffolk, and Essex."

"These counties of England are, at this very time, about as thickly peopled as the land of Canaan would have been with its population of Israelites only, without reckoning the aboriginal Canaanites, who already filled the land." "And surely it cannot be said that these three eastern counties, with their flourishing towns . . . . . and their innumerable villages, are in any danger of lying 'desolate,' with the beasts of the field multiplying against the human inhabitants."

This might pass for a tolerably clever sophistical puzzle; but, as an argument designed to produce conviction, it is weak enough. The fallacy lies in a dexterous confounding of the land promised to Israel with the land actually divided among the tribes by Joshua.

The territory granted to Israel may be likened to the early English colonies on this continent. The part originally settled, and from which the aboriginal inhabitants were first expelled, was a mere strip along the sea-coast; while the domain actually belonging to them was vastly more extensive, reaching, in the case of Israel, to the banks of the Euphrates, as in that of America to the shores of the Pacific. If an estimate were to be made of the population which the territory properly belonging to the United States is capable of supporting, Colenso could prove it to the last degree absurd by assuming that these hundreds of millions were to be crowded upon the acres of the thirteen states which formed the American Union.

In fact, if he will allow us a similar latitude, we can prove some of his own statements to be entirely 'unhistorical.' He tells us, on page 83, that "the entire population of the city of London was 2,362,236 by the census of 1851," and on page 87, that it is about "twelve miles square." We suppose him to refer to the vast metropolis so called, embracing, in addition to the city proper, that immense aggregation of suburbs which have become united with it. But suppose that we deal with him as he has done with Moses, and apply what he has said of London in its widest extent to London in its strict and narrower sense. By the census of 1851 the city of London proper contained 14,580 inhabited houses. Now if these are to hold the population, and cover the space which Colenso alleges, we must assign 162 occupants and upwards of six acres of ground to every house. Clearly there is something wrong, either in the English census or in the Bishop's method of reasoning.

We are sorry to be compelled to add, that his argument is as dishonest as it is unsound. The verse next succeeding those which he quotes, and upon which he comments so unfairly, defines the territory of which the Lord is speaking, Ex. xxiii. 31, 'And I will set thy bounds from the Red Sea, even unto the sea of the Philistines, and from the desert unto the river.' How can a man, with the least regard for truth, or even for his own reputation, ridicule a statement as manifestly false, because it is inapplicable to the narrow tract extending from the Mediterranean to just beyond the Jordan, when it is expressly declared to have reference to the territory bounded by the Red Sea and the desert on the South, the Mediterranean on the West, and the river Euphrates on the East?

Even if these limits were never set to the Holy Land elsewhere, yet they are in the passage under consideration. When the declaration was made that the former inhabitants should not be driven out in one year, lest 'the land become desolate, and the beast of the field multiply,' the extent of the land referred to was immediately defined to be as has just been stated. Why does the Bishop not even allude to this fact, in the course of his chapter, but base his whole argument on the assumption that a much more limited district is the one intended?

This is the more unpardonable, from the fact that this passage is not alone in fixing these boundaries for the promised land; but that the same limits are repeatedly assigned to it in other places. Thus the original grant to Abraham was, Gen. xv. 18, 'Unto thy seed have I given this land, from the river of Egypt unto the great river, the river Euphrates.' So Deut. xi. 24, 'From the wilderness and Lebanon, from the river, the river Euphrates, even unto the uttermost sea [viz. the Mediterranean] shall your coast be.' Josh. i. 4, 'From the wilderness and this Lebanon even unto the great river, the river Euphrates, all the land of the Hittites, and unto the great sea toward the going down of the sun, shall be your coast.'

But further, the territory promised to Israel exceeded that which was actually divided among the tribes by Joshua, not only in its breadth from East to West, but also in its length from North to South. Instead of reaching merely from Dan to Beersheba, it was to extend from the river of Egypt, Num. xxxiv. 5, or from the Red Sea, Ex. xxiii. 31, to the entrance of Hamath, Num. xxxiv. 8, Josh. xiii. 5. For our present purpose, it is needless to discuss the disputed and doubtful question of the precise position of this 'entrance to Hamath.' Whether we find it at the mouth of the Orontes, or in the depression at the northern end of Lebanon,* or at the city of Hamath itself, it still marks no small extension northward.

Now although it was not the divine purpose to put Israel in immediate possession of this extended territory, lest it should 'become desolate,' and although their own remissness obstructed their complete possession even of that portion which was at first divided amongst them, yet they did not forget the true extent of their claim.

* So Robinson, Later Biblical Researches, pp. 568, 569.

And hence we find David making war upon Hadad-ezer 'as he went to *recover his border* at the river Euphrates,' 2 Sam. viii. 3. And Jeroboam, the second of the name, is said, 2 Kin. xiv. 25, to have '*restored the coast of Israel* from the entering of Hamath to the sea of the plain.' It was, in fact, only in the most glorious period of the Hebrew State, in the reign of Solomon, that the promised land, in its divinely-prescribed limits, was really or substantially reduced to Israel's control. 'Solomon reigned over all kingdoms, from the river unto the land of the Philistines and unto the border of Egypt,' 1 Kin. iv. 21, 2 Chron. ix. 26. And in his days Israel held possession 'from the entering in of Hamath unto the river of Egypt,' 1 Kin. viii. 65, and even of a port upon the Red Sea, 1 Kin. ix. 26.

If the Bishop was bent upon bringing an objection from "the extent of the land of Canaan" at all hazards, the fact just adverted to would have supplied him with a much better one than he has adduced. He might have said, what has in fact been said by others, that the boundaries of the promised land, as described in the Pentateuch, are not those belonging to the days of Moses and Joshua, but those of the days of Solomon. Now as a map of the United States, which should include Texas, must have been prepared after the annexation of that state, so, it might be urged, a description of the boundaries of the land of Israel, as they were in the days of Solomon, could not have been written prior to his reign; and the existence of such a description, in writings ascribed to Moses, involves an anachronism which proves their spuriousness. This objection would have had a double advantage over the one which the Bishop has actually brought forward. In the first place, he would have escaped the necessity of a dishonest concealment of the facts; and in the second place, his objection would have been of some force from his rationalistic point of view.

To be sure, this objection would not, after all, be conclusive; but that is a difficulty arising out of the nature of things, and which those, who advocate the wrong side of a question, must make up their minds to experience. It would remain to be proved, that God, who sees the end from the beginning, could not make a promise to Abraham and to Moses, which he would fulfil to Solomon. And further, there is just enough difference between the ideal and the actual boundaries of Israel, the promise and its fulfilment, while justifying the substantial truth of the former, to prove that it is not merely an antedated copy of the latter, a *vaticinium ex eventu.* David and Solomon were at peace with the Sidonians, and entertained no thought of their conquest, 1 Kin. v. 1, 6, 12. On the other hand, David subdued Moab, 2 Sam. viii. 2, Ammon, ver. 12, and Edom, ver. 14. It is impossible that a sketch of Israel's boundaries, dating from that period, could have excluded Moab, Ammon, and Edom, Deut. ii. 5, 9, 19, and included the Sidonians, Judg. iii. 3; while it is quite natural that the altered circumstances of the time should have modified the limits prescribed ages before.

There is no escaping the conclusion, therefore, that limits were promised to the people under Moses and Joshua greater than they were enabled or permitted to occupy at that period, but which with unessential modifications, arising out of the subsequent course of events, they did occupy in the time of Solomon. The divine declaration, at which Colenso cavils, is thus abundantly verified. The fact is established beyond question, that the hostile nations were driven out by little and little, until Israel was increased and inherited the land; and that the promise of this result was given long before its actual accomplishment.

But Colenso might still object, that even within these enlarged boundaries two millions of people could have prevented the multiplication of wild beasts.

"The colony of Natal has an extent of 18,000 square miles, and a population, white and black included, probably not exceeding 150,000 altogether. This population is, of course, very scanty, and the land will allow of a much larger one. Yet the human inhabitants are perfectly well able to maintain their ground against the beasts of the field."

We do not know how it is at Natal, though the Bishop admits the existence of "leopards, wild boars, hyænas, and jackals," within the limits of his spiritual jurisdiction. We see it stated, however, in McCulloch's Universal Gazetteer, that the area of the province of Bengal is 82,700 square miles, and its population in 1822 was 24,887,000. This yields a proportion of 300 to the square mile, and is almost twice as densely peopled as the Bishop's own estimate makes Palestine to have been, and fully fifteen times more so than it would have been if Israel had at once taken possession of it up to the full limits of the promise. McCulloch further tells us—

"Tigers infest the jungles; and these with elephants, buffaloes, gyals, wild deer, and boars, jackals, apes of many kinds, etc., are natives of Bengal. . . . . . Crocodiles and gavials in the large rivers; the cobra-di-capello and other formidable serpents, etc."

Is McCulloch 'unhistorical' too, or is the argument valid only when applied to Moses?

The territory between the Jordan and the Euphrates, though spacious enough and productive enough to sustain several Syrian kingdoms in the days of David, was yet partly a wilderness, fitted chiefly for pasturage. The Bishop's figures are, therefore, deceptive for the additional reason that the inhabitants would not be uniformly distributed throughout; but while some parts of the land might be densely settled, other portions would contain a much more scanty population. The flocks of roving shepherds might be liable to the incursions of wild beasts, if the walled towns and cultivated farms were not.

And that this was not wholly an imaginary danger, appears from the frequent mention of wild animals in the sacred history, as the lion which encountered Samson in the vineyards of Timnath, Judg. xiv. 5; the lion and the bear which attacked the sheep of Jesse, 1 Sam. xvii. 34; the lion slain by one of David's champions, 2 Sam. xxiii. 20, and that which slew the unfaithful prophet, 1 Kin. xiii. 24; the bears, which tore in pieces the mocking children, 2 Kin. ii. 24; the lions sent among the heathen colonists planted in Samaria, 2 Kin. xviii. 25; and those which infested 'the swelling' of Jordan, even so late as the days of Jeremiah, xlix. 19, l. 44, not to speak of the period subsequent to the captivity, Zech. xi. 3. Even though every one of these incidents were dismissed as fabulous, the fact would remain; for such fables could not have arisen, nor could images drawn from these animals be so frequent in the prophets, and in the poetry of the bible, if they were not familiar in real life. Colenso may never have seen them in Natal, but they must have found their way into Palestine for all that.

CHAPTER XII.

THE NUMBER OF FIRST-BORNS COMPARED WITH THE NUMBER OF MALE ADULTS.

It is stated Num. iii. 43, that "all the first born males from a month old and upwards" were 22,273. As there were 600,000 males of twenty years and upwards, there must have been 900,000 or 1,000,000 males in all, and consequently but one first-born to forty or forty-four males.

"So that, according to the story in the Pentateuch, every mother in Israel must have had on the average forty-two sons!"

Again, if it be supposed that one-fourth of the first-borns had died before the numbering took place, and there were as many first-born females as males,

"there would then have been, if all had lived, about 60,000. But even this number of first-borns for a population of 1,800,000 would imply that each mother had on the average thirty children, fifteen sons and fifteen daughters. Besides which, the number of mothers must have been the same as that of the first-borns, male and female, including also any that had died. Hence there would have been only 60,000 child-bearing women to 600,000 men, so that only about one man in ten had a wife or children!"

These results are manifestly insupposable. But what is the conclusion, that Moses has blundered, or that his antagonist has mistaken his meaning? The latter anticipates (p. 148), that "by this time, surely, great doubt must have arisen in the mind of most readers, as to the historical veracity of sundry portions of the Pentateuch." As we have seen no cause to entertain any doubts of this sort as yet, while we have seen cause enough to doubt the infallibility of the Bishop, we are not prepared to discard the Hebrew legislator without inquiring a little further. We would not be willing to fasten such absurd conclusions as the Bishop draws, upon even a respectable writer of romance. His argument proves, what had been proved and confessed long before he was born, that there must be some mistake about the assumption that all the first-born males of the nation are reckoned in this enumeration. Moses, it is true, was directed to number all the first-born from a month old and upwards. But this must have been subject to some tacit limitation; and the difficulty is, in the absence of sufficient data, to determine what the nature and the ground of that limitation was.

There is some little doubt in the outset as to what would entitle a child to be called the first-born. If a man had children by several wives, for example, would he have one first-born, or more than one in his family? Upon the one side it is argued, that Jacob, Gen. xlix. 3, calls Reuben his first-born, as though there were but one entitled to that distinction, notwithstanding the fact, that children were born to him by four different mothers. Also when Reuben forfeited his right of primogeniture, this was devolved upon Joseph, 1 Chr. v. 1, as though that right could belong to but one in the family. So Deut. xxi. 15, in the case of a man having children by two wives, the one born first of all is declared to be the first-born. On the other hand it is urged from the form of expression used in the law of consecration, Ex. xiii. 2, 12, 15, that the first-born of every mother is here contemplated. The fact appears to have been that the paternal first-born was entitled to a double share of the inheritance ; but the consecration attached to the maternal first-born. The assumption of the prevalence of polygamy, therefore, even if there were any reliable grounds on which to base it, would rather complicate than relieve the matter.

There are three different opinions of greater or less plausibility as to the limitation to be put upon the enumeration of the first-born. The first is the very obvious one, that only those were to be reckoned, who were not themselves parents or heads of families. By the fact of their marriage they are withdrawn from the family to which they previously belonged, and form a new family of their own. They are accordingly regarded not in their former but in their present relation, not as the first-born of their fathers' families, but as the heads of their own. Kurtz, who adopts this view of the case, argues that marriages in the East take place on an average as early as the fifteenth or sixteenth year. With a population of 600,000 males over twenty years of age, there would probably be 200,000 under fifteen ; this would make one first-born for every nine males. Or, allowing that the number of females was equal to that of the males, there would be in 400,000 young people, 44,546 first-born, or one in every nine. This requires the assumption that there were nine children on an average in every Israelitish family. This is a large number, it is true, but perhaps not too great considering how prolific the Israelites are said to have been Ex. i. 7, 12, 20. This computation, the Bishop, fond as he is of figures when put by himself, omits, though professing to answer Kurtz's argument.

A second opinion is that of Baumgarten, and is based upon the redemption-money required of the supernumeraries. The 22,000 of the tribe of Levi were accepted in lieu of an equal number of the first-born in the other tribes. But for the redemption of the remaining 273, five shekels apiece were to be paid, Num. iii. 46, 47. This, according to Lev. xxvii. 6, was the amount fixed for the redemption of males "from a month old even unto five years old." Whence it appears to be not an unfair inference, that this was the limit of the ages of the first-born who were intended to be reckoned. The various stages of human life, as they are defined in this chapter of Leviticus, are under five years, between five and twenty, between twenty and sixty, and over sixty. It may have been understood that this enumeration was to be confined to the first stage of early childhood. If the fact be, as Bunsen alleges, that the surrounding heathen were in the habit of devoting their children to their idols when about this age, this is a coincidence which should not be overlooked. There might also be some historical reason for this limitation of which we are ignorant; as for example, it might have been five years since Moses was first sent to renew their covenant with God, and to prepare the way for their redemption, and the children born from that time onward might be claimed as holy unto the Lord.

A third opinion is perhaps more prevalent than either of the other two. It is that the law was not designed to be retro-active; but given as it was thirteen months before, at the time of instituting the passover on the eve of leaving Egypt, Ex. xiii. 2, 12–15, it has relation only to those who were subsequently born. This is inferred still further from Num. iii. 13, viii. 17, 'on the day that I smote all the first-born in the land of Egypt; I hallowed unto me all the first-born in Israel.' Thus Scott as quoted by Colenso:

"Upon reflection, we shall find it to be by no means improbable that among 1,200,000 persons of both sexes, who were above twenty years of age (and many might marry much younger than that age) there should be within that time [and, he might have added, the preceding year] 50,000 marriages; that is, about the twelfth part of the company of marriageable persons of each sex. Especially, if we consider that multitudes might be inclined to marry, when they found that they were about to enjoy liberty: and when they recollected that the promises made to Israel peculiarly respected a very rapid increase, and that there would doubtless be a very great blessing upon them in this respect."

Now, in our judgment, it would be a thousand-fold more reasonable to adopt any one of these explanations, than to suppose that either Moses or any other respectable writer would commit a blunder so gross as to assign forty-two sons to every mother in Israel, or to allow a wife and children to only one man in ten. If the Pentateuch were purely a fiction, we would expect more attention than this to the probabilities of the case, unless the writer of it was destitute of sense. The difficulty in the matter consists, as before stated, not in finding possible and plausible solutions, but in deciding in the absence of sufficient data which of these is the true one.

Colenso addresses himself to our ignorance when he alleges that no limitation in the ages of the first-born can be admitted, because none is expressly stated, and that as the Levites of all ages were to be numbered, so must the first-born be for whom they were to be substituted. Because we do not know what the limitation was, therefore there could be none, though the facts imperatively require it. If an agent of the Sunday School Union were to say in a public address that there were so many children in a given State or locality, he might, perhaps, intend to state the entire number of children of all ages, or he might mean all the children who were of an age to attend Sunday School. And if from statistics we found that the former could not be his meaning, we would not charge him with misrepresentation or with error for not having expressly mentioned a limitation, which he might suppose would be understood by his hearers. It is to set aside the very first principles of interpretation to say (p. 145) "the Hebrew usage has nothing to do with the present question. We are here only concerned with all the first-born." Hebrew usage has every thing to do with it. What we are concerned to know is precisely who were reckoned the first-born according to that usage and in the intent of the law requiring their consecration.

Much as such an acknowledgment would provoke the Bishop's scorn, we confess to such confidence in Moses and such reverence for his word, that even if these solutions should be proved to be impossible, which has never been done and cannot be done, we would still believe that there must be some other solution, though it has never yet been discovered. We heartily approve of the sentiment, which, as we had occasion to remark once before, the Bishop quotes with approbation (p. 16).

"We should be very scrupulous about assuming that it is impossible to explain satisfactorily this or that apparent inconsistency, contradiction, or other anomaly. . . . . considering that ours is an *ex parte* statement, and incapable of being submitted to the party against whom it is made."

In fact, sooner than charge the author of the Pentateuch with the absurdities which the Bishop, in the face of his own maxim, labours to fasten upon him, we would resort to the supposition that some transcriber, in the long period which has elapsed since the days of Moses, made an error in the figures. And we are confirmed in the view which we take of the matter by a curious circumstance in connection with this very enumeration which we are now considering. The Levites, who were accepted as substitutes for the first-born of the other tribes, were numbered at the same time. The census of each of the three Levitical families is first given, viz. the Gershonites 7,500, ver. 22, the Kohathites 8,600, ver. 28, the Merarites 6,200, ver. 34; then these are summed up and the number of the whole tribe stated to be 22,000, ver. 39. The true total is 22,300, leaving a discrepancy of 300 to be accounted for.

The Bishop may conclude from this that Moses was ignorant of the simplest rules of arithmetic. But few, we presume, will be disposed to follow him in doing so. Other inquirers have hit upon two solutions. One is that there is a mistake in the number through some error of transcription; and if this could take place in one instance, why not in another? A second solution is, that the 300 omitted in the final summation were the first-born of the tribe of Levi, who by the law were already consecrated themselves, and therefore could not stand as substitutes for the first-born in the other tribes. If this be so, 300 first-born in a tribe numbering 22,000 from a month old and upward, is a smaller proportion still than 22,273 in 900,000 or 1,000,000; and then we have here a fresh proof that there must have been some limitation of age in computing the first-born.

CHAPTER XIII.

THE SOJOURNING OF THE ISRAELITES IN EGYPT.

Ex. xii. 40. 'Now the sojourning of the children of Israel who dwelt in Egypt, was four hundred and thirty years.'

These words have been differently understood from very early times. The first impression, and that most naturally derived from them, is, that the children of Israel spent four hundred and thirty years in Egypt. Another very ancient interpretation, however, includes the migrations of their ancestors in Canaan as well as the abode in Egypt, in the period here given. As our author correctly informs us :—

"The Vatican copy of the LXX renders the passage thus: 'The sojourning of the children of Israel, which they sojourned *in Egypt and in the land of Canaan*, was 430 years.' The Alexandrian has, 'The sojourning of the children of Israel, which *they and their fathers* sojourned *in Egypt and in the land of Canaan*, was 430 years.' The Samaritan has, 'The sojourning of the *children of Israel and of their fathers*, which they sojourned *in the land of Canaan and in the land of Egypt*, was 430 years.'"

The gloss thus put upon this passage in Exodus, as it seemed to have the authority of an inspired apostle in its favour in Gal. iii. 17, and as the genealogy of Moses, Ex. vi. 16–20, appeared to preclude the supposition that 430 years were spent in Egypt, became the accepted and well nigh universal view of the case. It still has its advocates, though the leading biblical scholars of Europe have abandoned it.

It is so rare a thing to find Colenso standing fast by current and traditional opinions, that we are sorry to disturb his repose in the present instance. But, in fact, his concession to received views is from no lingering attachment to his ancient faith. If the 430 years embraced the peregrinations in Canaan as well as the abode in Egypt, only 210 or 215 years will remain for the latter; and then, as the Bishop proposes to show, (p. 148,) "the children of Israel, at the time of the Exodus, could not have amounted to two millions,—in fact, the whole body of warriors could not have been two thousand." A concession, made with such a view as this, may well provoke examination.

The Bishop tells us at the outset that the original words in this passage in Exodus—

"would be more naturally translated (as in the Vulgate, Chaldee, Syriac, and Arabic Versions) 'the sojourning of the children of Israel, *which they sojourned in Egypt*,' but for the serious difficulties which would thus arise."

The most serious difficulty, we apprehend, and that which was most influential with him, was that if he accepted this obvious sense of the words, his opportunity to cavil at the immense multiplication of the children of Israel would be cut off.

But what are "the serious difficulties" which he alleges?

"In the first place, St. Paul, referring to 'the covenant, that was confirmed before of God' unto Abraham, says 'the law,' which was *four hundred and thirty years after*, cannot disannul it,' Gal. iii. 17. It is plain, then, that St. Paul dates the beginning of the four hundred and thirty years, not from the going down into Egypt, but from the time of the promise made to Abraham."

We cannot help remarking upon the readiness here manifested to defer to the authority of an apostle as conclusive of the meaning of a passage in Exodus, when a few pages later he will not allow the like interference of another inspired writer in a similar instance. When a passage is adduced from Chronicles, which upsets a theory of his regarding certain statements of the Pentateuch, his reply is, (p. 157)—

> "We are not here concerned with the books of Chronicles . . . . but with the narrative in the Pentateuch itself and book of Joshua, and must abide by the data which they furnish."

We remember, however, that circumstances alter cases. We should not expect so good a reasoner as Colenso to be consistent. It is convenient to admit the testimony of inspiration this time, but it may not be agreeable to do it always.

This language of the apostle, however, does not appear to us to be decisive of the point at issue. The interval of time is only incidentally mentioned. Precision of statement regarding it was of no consequence to his argument. An opinion existed, and prevailed more or less widely, that it was but 430 years from the promise made to Abraham to the Exodus. It would not serve his present purpose to argue this point, or to make a categorical revelation respecting it. Enough was conceded on all hands to answer the end at which he was aiming. The interval was 430 years at least, as all confessed: whether it was more than this, he does not say, but leaves us to ascertain from other sources.

The evidence is, we think, conclusive, that the abode in Egypt lasted 430 years. This is the natural sense of Ex. xii. 40, and none would ever think of extracting a different meaning from it, but for reasons found outside of the verse itself. Abraham, Isaac, and Jacob were not 'children of Israel,' that their sojourning should be included; and the verse makes no allusion to Canaan, but only to Egypt. It was also revealed to Abraham, Gen. xv. 13, etc., that his seed should 'be a stranger in *a land that is not theirs*, and shall serve them, and they shall afflict them four hundred years . . . . . but in the fourth generation they shall come hither again.' The abode of the patriarchs in the land already promised to them is here positively excluded. They were to be strangers for four hundred years in a land not their own, and where they would be reduced to bondage, and suffer affliction. That this was not to take place until after Abraham's decease, appears from the contrast in ver. 15, 'and thou shalt go to thy fathers in peace; thou shalt be buried in a good old age.'

The prediction gives as the term of this foreign residence the round number 400 years: the record of the fulfilment states it with precision 430. Colenso himself yields the point, when he says, (p. 155,) that the fourth generation here spoken of can only be reckoned "from the time when they should leave the land of Canaan and go down into Egypt." The generation meant is a century, and 'the fourth generation' is a repetition in other terms of the 'four hundred years.'

The Bishop is able to find but one other "serious difficulty." This is the genealogy of Moses and Aaron in the sixth chapter of Exodus:

Ver. 16. 'And these are the names of the sons of Levi, according to their generations; Gershon, and Kohath, and Merari. And the years of the life of Levi were an hundred thirty and seven years.

17. 'The sons of Gershon . . . .

18. 'And the sons of Kohath; Amram, and Izhar, and Hebron, and Uzziel; and the years of the life of Kohath were an hundred and thirty and three years.

19. 'And the sons of Merari . . . .

20. 'And Amram took him Jochebed his father's sister to wife; and she bare him Aaron and Moses. And the years of the life of Amram were an hundred and thirty and seven years.

21. 'And the sons of Izhar. . . . .

22. 'And the sons of Uzziel. . . . .'

Upon this he makes the following remarks:—

"Now supposing that Kohath was only an *infant*, when brought down by his father to Egypt with Jacob, Gen. xlvi. 11, and that he begat Amram at the very end of his life, when 133 years old, and that Amram, in like manner, begat Moses, when he was 137 years old, still these two numbers added to 80 years, the age of Moses at the time of the Exodus, Ex. vii. 7, would only amount to 350 years, instead of 430.

"Once more, it is stated in the above passage, that 'Amram took him Jochebed his father's sister,'—Kohath's sister, and therefore Levi's daughter,—'to wife.' And so also we read Num. xxvi. 59: 'The name of Amram's wife was Jochebed, *the daughter of Levi, whom her mother bare to him in Egypt.*'

"Now Levi was one year older than Judah, and was therefore 43 years old when he went down with Jacob into Egypt; and we are told above, that he was 137 years old, when he died. Levi, therefore, must have lived, according to the story, 94 years in Egypt. Making here again the extreme supposition of his begetting Jochebed in the last year of his life, she may have been an infant 94 years after the migration of Jacob and his sons into Egypt. Hence it follows that, if the sojourn in Egypt was 430 years, Moses, who was 80 years old at the time of the Exodus, must have been born 350 years after the migration into Egypt, when his mother, even at the above extravagant supposition, must have been at the very least 256 years old."

Very well. But how does this genealogy agree with the alternative theory, which the Bishop has undertaken to defend, and which divides the years of sojourning between Egypt and Canaan. He confesses that this is "not without a strain upon one's faith." For even according to this hypothesis, Moses was born 80 years before the Exodus or 135 years after the migration into Egypt. And if Jochebed was born to Levi when he was 100 years old or 57 years after Jacob's migration, she would have been 78 when Moses was born.

Now as we do not think it safe to put the Bishop's faith to any more violent "strain" than is absolutely necessary, we hasten to relieve his mind of all difficulty even as to the longer term, by informing him that beyond all question some links have been omitted in tracing the line of Moses' descent.

It can scarcely be necessary to adduce proof to one who has even a superficial acquaintance with the genealogies of the Bible, that these are frequently abbreviated by the omission of unimportant names. In fact abridgment is the general rule, induced by the indisposition of the sacred writers to encumber their pages with more names than were necessary for their immediate purpose. This is so constantly the case, and the reason for it is so obvious, that the occurrence of it need create no surprise anywhere, and we are at liberty to suppose it whenever anything in the circumstances of the case favours that belief.

The omissions in the genealogy of our Lord as given in Matthew i., are familiar to all. Thus in ver. 8, three names are dropped between Joram and Ozias (Uzziah), viz. Ahaziah 2 Kings ix. 29, Joash 2 Kings xii. 1, and Amaziah 2 Kings xiv. 1; and in ver. 11 Jehoiakim is omitted after Josiah 2 Kings xxiii. 34, Chron. iii. 16. And in ver. 1, the entire genealogy is summed up in two steps "Jesus Christ, the son of David, the son of Abraham."

Other instances abound elsewhere; we mention only a few of the most striking. In 1 Chron. xxvi. 24 we read in a list of appointments made by King David (see 1 Chron. xxiv. 3, xxv. 1, xxvi. 26), that Shebuel,* the son of Gershom, the son of Moses, was ruler of the treasures; and again in 1 Chron. xxiii. 15, 16, we find it written 'The sons of Moses were Gershom and Eliezer. Of the sons of Gershom Shebuel was the chief.' Now with all Colenso's contempt for the "Chronicler," he can scarcely charge him with ignorance so gross as to suppose that the grandson of Moses could be living in the reign of David and appointed by him to a responsible office. Again in the same connection 1 Chron. xxvi. 31, 'among the Hebronites was Jerijah the chief;' and this Jerijah or Jeriah (for the names are identical,) was, xxiii. 19, the first of the sons of Hebron, and Hebron was ver. 12, the son of Kohath, the son of Levi, ver. 6. So that upon Colenso's principle of not allowing for any contraction in genealogical lists, we have the great-grandson of Levi holding a prominent office in the reign of David. Perhaps the Bishop can tell us, how old his mother must have been when he was born. Jochebed bearing Moses in her two hundred and fifty-sixth year would be nothing to it.

The genealogy of Ezra is recorded in the book which bears his name; but we learn from another passage, in which the same line of descent is given, that it has been

* He is called in 1 Chron. xxiv. 20, a son of Amram, the ancestor of Moses; for Shubael and Shebuel are in all probability mere orthographic variations of the same name.

abridged by the omission of six consecutive names. This will appear from the following comparison, viz:

1 Chron. vi. 3–14.	Ezra vii. 1–5.
1. Aaron	Aaron
2. Eleazar	Eleazar
3. Phinehas	Phinehas
4. Abishua	Abishua
5. Bukki	Bukki
6. Uzzi	Uzzi
7. Zerahiah	Zerahiah
8. Meraioth	Meraioth
9. Amariah	
10. Ahitub	
11. Zadok	
12. Ahimaaz	
13. Azariah	
14. Johanan	
15. Azariah	Azariah
16. Amariah	Amariah
17. Ahitub	Ahitub
18. Zadok	Zadok
19. Shallum	Shallum
20. Hilkiah	Hilkiah
21. Azariah	Azariah
22. Seraiah	Seraiah
	Ezra

Still further Ezra relates viii. 1–2:—

'These are now the chief of their fathers, and this is the genealogy of them that went up with me from Babylon, in the reign of Artaxerxes the King. Of the sons of Phinehas, Gershom. Of the sons of Ithamar, Daniel. Of the sons of David, Hattush.'

Here, according to the Bishop's principle of interpreting genealogies, we have a great-grandson and a grandson of Aaron, and a son of David coming up with Ezra from Babylon after the captivity. Now, though the Bishop, p. 157, by a stroke of his pen and without assigning any reason for it, decides that this book was "certainly composed long after the captivity," he can scarcely think its author so utterly ignorant of chronology as this would imply. Or if he were even prepared to go this length, such a conclusion is precluded by the more detailed genealogy of Hattush in 1 Chron. iii., see ver. 22, especially as he assigns the books of Chronicles to 'the same author who wrote the book of Ezra.'

This disposition to abbreviate genealogies by the omission of whatever is unessential to the immediate purpose of the writer is shown by still more remarkable reductions than those which we have been considering. Persons of different degrees of relationship are sometimes thrown together under a common title descriptive of the majority, and all words of explanation, even those which seem essential to the sense, are rigorously excluded, the supplying of these chasms being left to the independent knowledge of the reader. Hence several passages in the genealogies of Chronicles have now become hopelessly obscure. They may have been intelligible enough to contemporaries; but for those who have no extraneous sources of information, the key to their explanation is wanting. In other cases we are able to understand them, because the information necessary to make them intelligible is supplied from parallel passages of Scripture. Thus the opening verses of Chronicles contain the following bald list of names without a word of explanation, viz.:

'Adam, Sheth, Enosh, Kenan, Mahalaleel, Jered, Henoch, Methuselah, Lamech, Noah, Shem, Ham, and Japheth.'

We are not told who these persons are, how they were related to each other, or whether they were related. The writer presumes that his readers have the book of Genesis in their hands, and that the simple mention of these names in their order will be sufficient to remind them that the first ten trace the line of descent from father to son from the first to the second great progenitor of mankind; and that the last three are brothers, although nothing is said to indicate that their relationship is different from the preceding.

Again, the family of Eliphaz, the son of Esau, is spoken of in the following terms in 1 Chron. i. 36:

'The sons of Eliphaz: Teman and Omar, Zephi and Gatam, Kenaz and Timna, and Amalek.'

Now, by turning to Gen. xxxvi. 11, 12, we shall see that the first five are sons of Eliphaz, and the sixth his concubine, who was the mother of the seventh. This is so plainly written in Genesis, that the author of Chronicles, were he the most inveterate blunderer could not have mistaken it. But trusting to the knowledge of his readers to supply the omission, he leaves out the statement respecting Eliphaz's concubine, but at the same time connects her name and that of her son with the family to which they belong, and this though he was professedly giving a statement of the *sons* of Eliphaz.

So likewise in the pedigree of Samuel (or *Shemuel*, ver. 33, the difference in orthography is due to our translators, and is not in the original), which is given in 1 Chron. vi., in both an ascending and descending series. Thus in vs. 22–24:

'The sons of Kohath: Amminadab his son, Korah his son, Assir his son, Elkanah his son, and Ebiasaph his son, and Assir his son, Tahath his son, etc.'

The extent to which the framer of this list has studied comprehensiveness and conciseness will appear from the fact, which no one would suspect unless informed from other sources, that while the general law which prevails in it is that of descent from father to son, the third, fourth, and fifth names are brothers. This is shown by a comparison of Ex. vi. 24, and the parallel genealogy, 1 Chron. vi. 36, 37. So that the true line of descent is the following, viz.:

	In vs. 22–24		In vs. 37, 38
	Kohath		Kohath
	Amminadab		Izhar
	Korah		Korah
Assir, Elkanah,	Ebiasaph		Ebiasaph
	Assir		Assir
	Tahath, etc.		Tahath, etc.

The circumstance that the son of Kohath is called in one list Amminadab, and in the other Izhar, is no real discrepancy and can create no embarrassment, since it is no unusual thing for the same person to have two names. Witness Abram and Abraham, Jacob and Israel, Joseph and Zaphnath-paaneah, Gen. xli. 45, Oshea, Jehoshua, Num. xiii. 16 (or Joshua) and Jeshua, Neh. viii. 17, Gideon and Jerŭbbaal, Judg. vi. 32, Solomon and Jedidiah, 2 Sam. xii. 24, 25, Azariah and Uzziah, 2 Kin. xv. 1. 13, Daniel and Belteshazzar, Hananiah, Mishael, Azariah and Shadrach, Meshach, Abednego, Dan. i. 7; Saul and Paul, Thomas and Didymus, Cephas and Peter, and in profane history Cyaxares and Darius, Octavianus and Augustus, Napoleon and Buonaparte, Ferretti and Pius IX., Colenso and Natal (p. 37).

We think that with these facts before him it would be putting no undue strain upon the Bishop's 'faith' to ask him to admit that the genealogy of Moses may have been condensed, as so many others have been, by the dropping of some of the less important names. The question, with which we are concerned, is not how the Bishop would have constructed a genealogy, nor how in his opinion the Hebrews ought to have kept their genealogies, or inspired men ought to have recorded them, but what are the facts? What is the structure of the genealogies actually found in the Scriptures? And inasmuch as names, which would be a needless incumbrance, are so frequently passed over; why may not that be the case in the present instance?*

We need not content ourselves, however, with a pos-

* We may here be indulged with a remark aside from the special topic before us, viz.: that if scientific research should ever demonstrate what it cannot be said to have done as yet, that the race of man has existed upon the earth for a longer period than the ordinary Hebrew Chronology will allow, we would be disposed to seek the solution in this frequent, if not pervading, characteristic of the Scriptural genealogies. The Septuagint chronology, to which many have fled in their desire to gain the additional centuries which it allots to human history, is, we are persuaded, a broken reed. The weight of evidence preponderates immensely in favour of the correctness of the Hebrew text, and against the accuracy of the deviations of the Septuagiut. But it must not be forgotten that there is an element of uncertainty in a computation of time which rests upon genealogies, as the sacred chronology so largely does. Who is to certify us that the ante-diluvian and ante-Abrahamic genealogies have not been condensed in the same manner as the post-Abrahamic? If Matthew omitted names from the ancestry of our Lord in order to equalize the three great periods over which he passes, may not Moses have done the same in order to bring out seven generations from Adam to Enoch, and ten from Adam to Noah? Our current chronology is based upon the *primâ facie* impression of these genealogies. This we shall adhere to, until we see good reason for giving it up. But if these recently discovered indications of the antiquity of man, over which scientific circles are now so excited, shall, when carefully inspected and thoroughly weighed, demonstrate all that any have imagined they might demonstrate, what then? They will simply show that the popular chronology is based upon a wrong interpretation, and that a select and partial register of ante-Abrahamic names has been mistaken for a complete one.

sibility or a probability; we have the means of arriving at positive certainty. This is afforded us in the first place by parallel genealogies of the same period, as that of Bezaleel, 1 Chron. ii. 18–20, which records seven generations from Jacob, and that of Joshua, 1 Chron. vii. 23–27, which records eleven. Now, it is not conceivable without a very severe 'strain upon one's faith,' that there should be eleven links in the line of descent from Jacob to Joshua, and only four from Jacob to Moses.

A still more convincing proof is yielded by Num. iii. 19, 27, 28, from which it appears that the four sons of Kohath severally gave rise to the families of the Amramites, the Izeharites, the Hebronites, and the Uzzielites; and that the number of the male members of these families of a month old and upward was 8,600 one year after the Exodus. So that if no abridgment has taken place in the genealogy, the grandfather of Moses had in the lifetime of the latter 8,600 descendants of the male sex alone, 2,750 of them being between the ages of thirty and fifty, Num. iv. 36.

It may suit the purposes of Colenso (p. 170), to attempt to fasten such a glaring Munchausenism as this upon the author of the Pentateuch. But persons of a more sober judgment will conclude that whether the Pentateuch is a history or a fiction, this cannot be its meaning; and they will prefer to avoid this incredible result by assuming that the genealogy of Moses is constructed upon the same principle of condensation, which prevails to so great an extent in those, which are found in other parts of Scripture. Is there anything, then, in the structure of this genealogy to preclude so necessary an assumption?

It might appear at first sight as though there was, and

as though the letter of it shut us up to the inevitable conclusion that there were four links and no more from Jacob to Moses. The names which we find without deviation in all the genealogies, are Jacob, Levi, Kohath, Amram, Moses, Ex. vi. 16–20, Num. iii. 17–19, xxvi. 57–59, 1 Chron. vi. 1–3, 16–18, xxiii. 6–12–13. Now unquestionably Levi was Jacob's own son. So likewise Kohath was the son of Levi, Gen. xlvi. 11, and born before the descent into Egypt. Amram also was the immediate descendant of Kohath; it is not possible, as Kurtz proposes, to insert the missing links between them. For in the first place according to Num. xxvi. 59, 'the name of Amram's wife was Jochebed, the daughter of Levi, whom her mother bare to Levi in Egypt,' this Jochebed being, Ex. vi. 20, 'his father's sister.' Now while a 'daughter of Levi' might have the general sense of a descendant of Levi, as the woman healed by our Lord, Luke xiii. 16, is called a 'daughter of Abraham,' the words which follow are too specific to admit of this interpretation. A daughter *born to Levi in Egypt* naturally suggests the contrast of members of his family born before he left Canaan, and seems to confine the meaning to one of Levi's own children. Kurtz proposes to rid himself of this troublesome expression by assuming that it is an interpolation. But that is an extreme measure, not to be resorted to except in cases of absolute necessity. Jochebed, therefore, was Levi's own daughter, and the sister of Kohath, who must accordingly have been Amram's own father. And secondly, Amram was, Num. iii. 27, the father of one of the four subdivisions of the Kohathites, these subdivisions springing from Kohath's own children, and comprising together 8,600 male descendants. Moses' father surely could not have been the ancestor of one-fourth of this number in Moses' own days.

To avoid this difficulty Tiele* and Keil† assume that there were two Amrams, one the son of Kohath, another, who was a more remote descendant but bore the same name with his ancestor, the father of Moses. This relieves the embarrassment created by the Amramites, Num. iii. 27, but is still liable to that which arises from making Jochebed the mother of Moses. And further the structure of the genealogy in Ex. vi. is such as to make this hypothesis unnatural and improbable. Verse 16 names the three sons of Levi, Gershon, Kohath, and Merari; vers. 17–19 the sons of each in their order; vers. 20–22 the children of Kohath's sons; vers. 23–24 contain descendants of the next generation, and ver. 25 the generation next following. Now according to the view of Tiele and Keil we must either suppose that the Amram, Izhar and Uzziel of vers. 20–22 are all different from the Amram, Izhar and Uzziel of ver. 18, or else that Amram though belonging to a later generation than Izhar and Uzziel, is introduced before them, which the regular structure of the genealogy forbids, and besides the sons of Izhar, and the sons of Uzziel who are here named, were the contemporaries of Moses and Aaron the sons of Amram, Num. xvi. 1, Lev. x. 4.

This subject may be relieved from all perplexity, however, by observing that Amram and Jochebed were not the immediate parents, but only the ancestors of Aaron and Moses. How many generations may have intervened we cannot tell. It is indeed said Ex. vi. 20, Num. xxvi. 59, that Jochebed bare them to Amram; but in

* Das erste Buch Moses, p. 409, etc.

† Biblischer Commentar über die Bucher Mose's I. p, 350.

the language of genealogies this simply means that they were descended from her and from Amram. Thus in Gen. xlvi. 18, after recording the sons of Zilpah, her grandsons and her great-grandsons, the writer adds, 'These are the sons of Zilpah . . . . and these *she bare unto Jacob*, even sixteen souls.' The same thing recurs in the case of Bilhah, ver. 25: '*she bare these unto Jacob;* all the souls were seven.' Compare vers. 15, 22. No one can pretend here that the author of this register did not use the term understandingly of descendants beyond the first generation. In like manner according to Mat. i. 11, Josias begat his grandson Jechonias, and ver. 8, Joram begat his great-great-grandson Ozias. And in Gen. x. 15–18 Canaan, the grandson of Noah, is said to have begotten several whole nations, the Jebusite, the Amorite, the Girgasite, the Hivite, etc., etc. Nothing can be plainer, therefore, than that in the usage of the Bible, 'to bear' and 'to beget' are used in a wide sense to indicate descent, without restricting this to the immediate offspring.

Nothing, therefore, obliges us to regard Amram and Jochebed as the immediate parents of Aaron and Moses, unless it be that, Lev. x. 4, Uzziel, Amram's brother, is called 'the uncle (דּוֹד) of Aaron.' But, in fact, the Hebrew דּוֹד, like the English *cousin* (from *consanguineus*), though often specifically applied to a definite degree of relationship, has, both from etymology and usage, a much wider sense. Accordingly, דּוֹד, Jer. xxxii. 12, has the same meaning as בֶּן־דּוֹד, ver. 8, showing that it may mean *cousin* as well as *uncle*. But, though the word were restricted in its significance to a *father's brother*, it must still, of necessity, have a range equal to that of *father* itself, and denote in general the brother of a paternal ancestor. A great-great-grand-uncle is still an uncle, and would be properly described by the term דּוֹד.

It may also be observed, that in the actual history of the birth of Moses his parents are not called Amram and Jochebed. It is simply said, Ex. ii. 1: 'And there went a man of the house of Levi and took to wife a daughter of Levi.'

If it be asked, why were just these three remote ancestors of Moses named, and his more immediate progenitors omitted? the answer is, that these characterized with sufficient accuracy the line of descent to which he belonged. He was of the tribe of Levi, of the family of Kohath, and of that division of the family which was descended from Amram. To one familiar with the tribal system of Israel this described everything that was essential. Princeton, New Jersey, U. S. A., would be a sufficient designation of the place where we are writing, without the necessity of inserting the minuter divisions of township and county. The lineage of the present sovereign of Great Britain would be sufficiently indicated, and her claim to the throne exhibited, by pointing out that she is sprung from the house of Hanover, and this from the Stuarts, and the Stuarts from the Plantagenets, the Plantagenets from the Tudors, and the Tudors from the house of Normandy. That Victoria is the rightful heiress of George I., who was descended from James I., who was descended from Henry VII., who was descended from Henry II., who was descended from William the Conqueror, tells the whole story. Her line of descent is completely traced without the insertion of another name.

The conclusion of the whole matter, therefore, is that the genealogy of Moses and Aaron interposes no obstacle to understanding Ex. xii. 40, as Colenso tells us it may 'more naturally' be understood. And as this is the last of the 'serious difficulties' of which he speaks, in the way of this more natural interpretation, we cannot but think that the way is open for him to adopt it without any further 'strain upon his faith.' Israel was 430 years in Egypt.

CHAPTER XIV.

THE EXODUS IN THE FOURTH GENERATION.

Colenso understands the declaration, Gen. xv. 16, 'in the fourth generation they shall come hither again,' to mean that the descendants of the patriarchs at the fourth remove from those who went down into Egypt, should leave the land of their oppression. He nowhere intimates that the expression has ever been understood, or can possibly be understood, in any other way. If he had studied Kurtz as carefully as he professes to have done, he ought to have learned that the term 'generation' is often used to denote the entire body of contemporary men, and that its duration is measured by the length of human life. Thus, it is said, Ex. i. 6: 'And Joseph died, and all his brethren, and all that generation;' although Joseph's life was extended to four generations, in the narrower sense of the term, for he saw his son Ephraim's great-grandsons, Gen. l. 23. A hundred years is not too long an estimate for a generation at that period, and in that case the fourth generation will be coincident with the 400 years, ver. 12, during which Abraham's seed was to be 'a stranger in a land that is not theirs.'

But the Bishop undertakes to confirm his view of the case in the following manner·

"If we examine the different genealogies of remarkable men, which are given in various places of the Pentateuch, we shall find that, as a rule, the contemporaries of Moses and Aaron are descendants in the *third*, and those of Joshua and Eleazar in the *fourth* generation, from some one of the *sons*, or *adult grandsons*, of Jacob, who went down with him into Egypt. Thus we have:—

	1st Gen.	2d Gen.	3d Gen.	4th Gen.	5th Gen.	
Levi.....	Kohath	Amram	Moses	....	....	Ex. vi. 16, 18, 20.
Levi.....	Kohath	Amram	Aaron	....	....	Ex. vi. 16, 18, 20.
Levi.....	Kohath	Uzziel	Mishael	....	....	Lev. x. 4.
Levi.....	Kohath	Uzziel	Elzaphan	....	....	Lev x. 4.
Levi.....	Kohath	Izhar	Korah	....	....	Num. xvi. 1.
Reuben ..	Pallu	Eliab	Dathan	....	....	Num. xxvi. 7–9.
Reuben ..	Pallu	Eliab	Abiram	....	....	Num. xxvi. 7–9.
Zarah....	Zabdi	Carmi	Achan	....	....	Josh. vii. 1.
Pharez...	Hezron	Ram	Amminadab	Nahshon	....	Ruth iv. 18, 19.
Pharez...	Hezron	Segub	Jair	....	....	1 Ch. ii. 21, 22.
Pharez...	Hezron	Caleb	Hur	Uri	Bezaleel	1 Ch. ii. 18–20."

Upon this tabular exhibit we may remark first, that the measure of correspondence which appears in it is in part produced by forcing. While the first seven are counted from the sons of Jacob, the last four are reckoned from his grandsons. Nahshon would be the fifth, and Bezaleel the sixth from Judah; or, if the other mode of reckoning be adopted, Moses, Aaron, etc., would be the second from Kohath. It is too bad for the Bishop to try to impose upon his readers by the remark, that

"Hezron, as well as his father, Pharez, was born, according to the story, in the land of Canaan; so that Bezaleel was actually still in the fourth generation from one who went down into Egypt."

The very first difficulty which he alleges in the Mosaic narrative, and to which he devotes two chapters, is that Hezron, "*according to the story*," could not have been born in the land of Canaan. With the best disposition to accommodate the Bishop, we cannot suffer him to stand on both sides of the same fence. Secondly, the correspondence would be still further destroyed by including Zelophehad,* Num. xxvii. 1, the fifth, and Joshua, 1 Chron. vii. 22–27, the tenth from Joseph. Thirdly, it has already been shown that the genealogy of Moses and Aaron is abridged, by omitting some of their more immediate ancestors. The same argument is valid for Mishael, Elzaphan, and Korah, and, to say the least, creates a probability that the same is the case with the rest. Fourthly, that the genealogy in which Nahshon stands has been similarly condensed, is susceptible of ready proof. His grandson, Boaz, Ruth iv. 21, 22, was the son of Rahab, Matt. i. 5, and the great-grandfather of David. As Rahab was a woman in mature life at the time of the miraculous passage of the Jordan, and it was about 360 years† from that event to the birth of David, some names must have been dropped from the genealogy

* If it were not for the Bishop's arithmetical pedantry and his incessant display of figures, we would take no notice of the following slip, which need create no surprise, however, since even *bonus dormitat Homerus.*

"If the sojourn in Egypt had lasted 430 years, instead of 210 or 215, then 360 years must have intervened between the birth of Gilead and the Exodus; and we should have to suppose that Gilead had a son, Hepher, when 180 years old, and Hepher also had a son, Zelophehad, when 180 years old, that so Zelophehad might even have been born at the time of the Exodus, and been able to have full-grown daughters, as the story implies, at the end of the forty years' wanderings."

But why must Zelophehad be just 'born at the time of the Exodus?' He may have been, for all that appears, forty years of age, or older still, and then his father and grandfather need only have been 160 at the birth of their respective children. The author of an arithmetic ought to have been more exact.

† From 1 Kings vi. 1 it appears that the 4th year of Solomon's reign was the 480th after the departure from Egypt; from this must be deducted the 40 years spent in the wilderness, the length of David's life, which is not certainly known, and 4 years of the reign of Solomon.

or else each parent was on an average between 90 and 100 years old at the birth of his child. Fifthly, the genealogy of Moses and Aaron, Ex. vi. 16–20, doubtless contains an allusion to God's promise to Abraham, that his seed should return to Canaan in the fourth generation. This is to be found, not in the number of its links, but in the indication which it affords of their length. We are told, ver. 16, that the years of the life of Levi were 137, ver. 18, those of Kohath, 133, ver. 20, those of Amram, 137. We have before estimated these generations at 100 years each; if, upon the evidence furnished by this genealogy, we reckon them at 130, then three generations would be 390 years. And in the fourth generation the people not only left Egypt, but completed their wanderings in the desert, and actually entered the promised land. So that the language of Gen. xv. 16 is precisely verified.

The genealogy of Joshua, 1 Chron. vii. 22–27, is so troublesome to our author that he sets himself to get rid of it at all hazards. He first shows that upon his estimate of the abode in Egypt, there would not be time for ten generations from Joseph to Joshua; and then instead of concluding that his estimate is wrong insists that the genealogy is incredible.

"Again, according to the chronicler, 'Elishama, the son of Ammihud,' was the grandfather of Joshua. But 'Elishama, the son of Ammihud,' was himself the captain of the host of Ephraim, Num. ii. 18, about a year after his *grandson*, Joshua, had commanded the whole Hebrew force which fought with Amalek, Ex. xvii. 8–16, which also is hardly credible."

We find no difficulty in believing that a man and his grandfather might both be in active duty at the same time; and we are surprised that it should trouble Colenso, when on the very next page he argues from it as a fact that Joseph was living at the birth of Ammihud, his great-great-grandson, Gen. l. 23.

"In vers. 22, 23, we have this most astonishing fact stated, that Ephraim himself, after the slaughter by the men of Gath of his descendants in the *seventh* generation, 'mourned many days,' and then married again, and had a son Beriah, who was the *ancestor of Joshua!*'

The passage on which he professes to base this most extraordinary and absurd misrepresentation is the following:

"And the sons of Ephraim: Shuthelah and Bered his son, and Tahath his son, and Eladah his son, and Tahath his son, and Zabad his son, and Shuthelah his son, and Ezer and Elead, whom the men of Gath that were born in that land slew, because they came down to take away their cattle. And Ephraim their father mourned many days, and his brethren came to comfort him. And when he went in to his wife, she conceived and bare a son, and he called his name Beriah, because it went evil with his house."

There is a possible corroboration of the circumstance here referred to in 1 Chron. viii. 13, whence it appears that certain descendants of Benjamin, ancestors of the subsequent settlers in Ajalon, 'drove away the inhabitants of Gath.' But apart from this, Ezer and Elead, who were slain, were not sons of the seventh generation, but the immediate children of Ephraim, and are to be connected directly with the first Shuthelah, the intervening names which trace the descent from Shuthelah forming a parenthesis. Bertheau, whose proclivities are anything but favourable to the truth and inspiration of the Scripture history, and who gives a mythical explanation of this very passage, nevertheless remarks upon it in his commentary on Chronicles:

"The descendants of Shuthelah are traced through seven generations, in which the name Shuthelah recurs and the name Tahath is found twice

The two, which are named last, Ezer and Elead, must be regarded as sons of Ephraim and continue the series begun with Shuthelah, in ver. 20."

Such reckless misstatements on the part of the Bishop, compel us to think, that he has adopted a very singular mode of propitiating the "strong practical love of truth in his fellow-countrymen, whether Clergy or Laity," to which as he declares (p. 18) he makes his appeal.

The Targum relates, that Ezer and Elead were the victims of a premature and unsuccessful attempt to take Palestine, into which they were betrayed by a misinterpretation of the promise to Abraham. We are not able to verify the truth of this tradition; but it would be curious if these sons of Ephraim had fallen into the Bishop's mistake of reckoning the four generations as four links in the chain of descent—Jacob—Joseph—Ephraim—Ezer—and paid the penalty of their error with their lives.

CHAPTER XV.

THE NUMBER OF ISRAELITES AT THE TIME OF THE EXODUS.

"The twelve sons of Jacob had between them 53 sons, that is, on the average 4½ each. Let us suppose that they increased in this way from generation to generation. Then in the *first* generation, that of *Kohath*, there would be 54 males, (according to the story, 53, or rather only 51, since Er and Onan died in the land of Canaan, *v.* 12, without issue,)—in the *second*, that of *Amram*, 243,—in the *third*, that of *Moses* and *Aaron*, 1,094,—and in the *fourth*, that of *Joshua* and *Eleazar*, 4,923; that is to say, instead of 600,000 warriors in the prime of life, there could not have been 5,000."

Upon this we remark in the first place, that if this result be accepted, the difficulty will only be shifted without being removed. It has been seen in a former chapter, that nothing is more certain in the history of Israel, than that the people emigrated from Egypt to the promised land, and took possession of the latter by the forcible expulsion of its former occupants. Now if Joshua accomplished this with but five thousand men, he must have been attended with such a divine blessing as could with equal ease have effected a miraculous multiplication of the people in Egypt.

Secondly, The ratio of increase, which is assumed, is based on a very limited survey of facts, and these not impartially selected but artfully chosen from such as are most favourable to the result which it is desired to establish. If Jacob's own family of twelve sons had been made the standard, his 53 grandsons would have had 1,099,008 male descendants of the fourth generation alone, not to speak of those surviving from preceding generations; and 1,000,000 males is all that Colenso himself supposes that the account in Exodus calls for. Besides, his estimate is derived from the state of things during the period of waiting and of expectancy, and not that of the actual fulfilment of the promise. In order to train the faith of the patriarchs, the chosen seed was during the first stage of its existence restricted to a very slender increase. The proper time for it to develope itself to a nation did not begin till Jacob went down into Egypt. A man plants a young apple tree, and in its fourth year perhaps gathers two or three apples from it. Here Colenso would come in with his Arithmetic and say, 'If it yields three apples in four years, how long will it take to yield a bushel?' The owner of the tree would probably reply to his calculations, that its bearing season had not yet come.

Thirdly, the assumption of but four generations in the sense here put upon the term from the descent into Egypt to the Exodus is an error, as was shown in the last chapter. Even upon the theory that the children of Israel were but 215 years in Egypt, this requires 72 years for a generation, for Colenso counts Jacob's grandsons who went down with him the first, and those of the age of Joshua and Eleazar the fourth. But let this pass. The children of Israel were 430 years in Egypt instead of 215. Double the number of generations, and at the rate of increase which he adopts himself, the males of the eighth generation will amount to 2,018,786, twice as many consequently as the account in Exodus requires for all the males then living.

In order to set the statements of Moses in a still more unfavourable light, the following hypothesis is suggested:—

"Supposing the 51 males of the *first* generation (Kohath's) to have had each on the average three sons, and so on, we shall find the number of males in the *second* generation (Amram's) 153, in the *third* (Aaron's) 459, and in the *fourth* (Eleazar's) 1377,—instead of 600,000."

But according to the Bishop's own figures Moses is correct again, if we bear in mind that the residence in Egypt lasted 430 years and allow 48 years, which is surely long enough, for a generation. Then counting Kohath's generation the first, the tenth generation alone* without allowing for any survivors from those which preceded it would amount to 1,043,199 males.

In a subsequent chapter (pp. 172, 173,) he presents another view of the case.

"Assume that the Hebrew population increased, like that of England, at the rate of 23 per cent. in 10 years, then reckoning the males as about half the entire population,† we shall find that the 51 males in Gen. xlvi. would have only increased in 215 years to 4,375, instead of 1,000,000."

If we correct this estimate by substituting 430 years in place of 215, and 66 as the number of male-members of Jacob's family who went down into Egypt in place of 51, we shall find that even upon the rate of increase in an old and populous country like England, the Israelites would

* According to 1 Chron. vii. 22–27, Joshua was the tenth, as Ephraim was the first, from Joseph. If any links have been omitted from the genealogy, as is possible, to say the least, he belonged to a later generation still.

† No allowance is made for this in the Bishop's calculation; the number, which he gives, represents the males simply, and must be doubled if the entire population is demanded. And the algebraic formula for its determination is not $51\ (1.23)^{21\frac{1}{2}}$ as he states it, but $2 \times 51\ (1.23)^{21\frac{1}{2}}$

have amounted to 484,689 males at the time of the Exodus. If, however, we adopt instead the rate of increase in the United States, which on an average from 1790 to 1850 was 34½ per cent. every ten years, they would have amounted to the prodigious number of 22,625,739 males, which is 22 times greater than the account in Exodus requires us to suppose. It does not seem, therefore, that the statements of Moses are so incredible after all.

The theory of the growth of population is a very intricate subject, and involves many difficult and delicate questions. In order to treat the multiplication of the Israelites in Egypt understandingly, we would need to be informed minutely of many things in their condition and habits of life, of which we are profoundly ignorant. It cannot be dismissed, however, by imperiously pronouncing it impossible. The considerations already presented, drawn from computations which Colenso himself allows, or from modern analogies patent to all, are sufficient to show, that there is no natural impossibility in the case. The precise course of things we cannot trace in all its steps for each of the requisite data. The following estimate by Keil,* presents a moderate and rational view of the case upon the basis of the facts as recorded.

"If we deduct from the seventy souls, who went down into Egypt, the patriarch Jacob, his twelve sons, Dinah, and Serah the daughter of Asher, and in addition the three sons of Levi, the four grandsons of Judah and Benjamin [Asher?] and those grandsons of Jacob who probably died without male offspring, inasmuch as their descendants do not occur among the families of Israel (see Num. xxvi.), there will remain forty-one grandsons of Jacob (besides the Levites) who founded families. If now, according to 1 Chron. vii. 20, etc., where ten or eleven generations are

---

* Biblischer Commentar über die Bücher Mose's, I. p. 392.

named from Ephraim to Joshua, we reckon forty years to a generation, the tenth generation of the forty-one grandsons of Jacob would be born about the 400th year of the residence in Egypt, and consequently be about twenty years old at the Exodus. Supposing that in the first six of these generations every married couple had on an average three sons and three daughters, and in the last four generations each married couple had two sons and two daughters, there would have been in the tenth generation, about the 400th year after the descent into Egypt, 478,224 sons, who could be over twenty years of age at the Exodus, whilst 125,326 men of the ninth generation might be still living, and consequently, 478,224 + 125,326 = 603,550 men over twenty years old could leave Egypt."

Besides what has already been said, three additional considerations should be taken into the account in estimating the Mosaic record upon this subject.

The first is, the promised blessing of God. Colenso, indeed, ventures the statement, (p. 162.)

"We have no reason whatever, from the data furnished by the sacred books themselves, to assume that they had families materially larger than those of the present day."

And after having said this he tells us four pages later, that according to the data of the sacred books "we must suppose that each man had forty-six children (twenty-three of each sex), and each of these twenty-three sons had forty-six children, and so on!" This is of course a grievous misrepresentation; but it is in the face of his own words nevertheless.

The burden of the promises to the patriarchs was the immense multiplication of their seed, Gen. xiii. 16, xxii. 17, xlvi. 3. And how marvellously these were fulfilled, appears not only from the actual numbers as they are recorded, but from such statements as Ex. i. 7. 'And the children of Israel were fruitful, and increased abundantly, and multiplied, and waxed exceedingly mighty; and the land was filled with them.' And though this surprising increase excited the jealous hostility of the king of Egypt, and measures were adopted to check it, these were without avail. Ver. 12, 'The more they afflicted them, the more they multiplied and grew,' ver. 20. 'The people multiplied and waxed very mighty.'

The second consideration is, that it has been tacitly assumed thus far, that all of Jacob's descendants, who were living at the time of going down into Egypt, were included in the seventy souls, Gen. xlvi. 27. But in all probability he had daughters and granddaughters, who are not named in this list. On this point Colenso observes:

> "It is certainly strange that, among all the sixty-nine children and grandchildren, and great-grandchildren of Jacob, who went down with him into Egypt, there should be only *one* daughter mentioned, and one granddaughter. The very numbering of these two among the 'seventy souls' shows that the females 'out of the loins of Jacob' were not omitted *intentionally*."
>
> "It is certain that the writer intends it to be understood that these seventy were the *only* persons, and these *two* the only females, who had at that time been born in the family of Jacob. And though the fact itself of this wonderful preponderance of males may seem very strange, and would be so indeed in actual history; it is only another indication of the unhistorical character of the whole account."

We are of the Bishop's opinion so far as this, that we too would think it very strange, if among sixty-nine children and grandchildren there was but one daughter, and one granddaughter. We are also inclined to go with him one step further, and think that this could not have been so. But we differ from him in this, that we do not believe that Moses meant to represent that it was so. Especially after what Colenso himself tells us of another family register, though he at the same time tries to save the credit of his former unproved statement by dint of confident assertion:

"The females appear to be omitted purposely in Ex. vi. (as we see by the omission of Amram's [Levi's?] daughter, Jochebed), *though they could not have been omitted* in Gen. xlvi., as we have seen above."

If Jochebed's name could be "omitted purposely" in the account of Levi's children, Ex. vi. 16, why may the names of daughters not have been omitted elsewhere? And why is it not more reasonable to suppose that they were omitted purposely, than to declare the "whole account" "unhistorical," because such names do not appear? In all the genealogies of the Bible very few daughters are mentioned, and whenever any are spoken of, it always appears to be for some special reason. The rule is, to omit them for the reason that they were not regarded as constituting heads of families. And hence, Num. xxvii. 4, the daughters of Zelophehad feared that the name of their father would 'be done away from among his family, because he had no son.'

That a like omission occurred in Jacob's family register, Gen. xlvi., is probable, 1st. From the general analogy of genealogies and family lists already mentioned. 2d. From the omission of other female members of the family, as Jacob's sons' wives, ver. 26. 3d. This is perhaps intimated in ver. 23, 'and the sons of Dan, Hushim.' The plural 'sons' seems to imply that Dan had more than one child, and yet only one is mentioned; why were the others omitted, unless because they were daughters? The choice lies between this understanding of it, and supposing that he had one or more sons subsequently born in Egypt, or that the plural 'sons' is used instead of the singular.

The fact that a daughter and granddaughter are mentioned does not prove that others were not passed over. There may have been special reasons, why these should not be named which did not apply to the rest. Dinah's unhappy notoriety might account for the mention of the name. Or, there may be a designed significance in including one daughter, probably the first, of each generation in this primary register of Israel. As we have seen that there was a symbolic meaning in its number seventy, is it too much to imagine that these two specimen names taken from among the female members of Jacob's household had a mystic import too? These also are of Israel. As the number seventy points forward to the time when there shall be 'neither Jew nor Greek,' may not this other feature of the register have been intended to prefigure the great gospel fact that 'there is neither male nor female; for ye are all one in Christ Jesus?' Gal. iii. 28.

A third consideration is, that the household or retinue of the patriarch was still further enlarged by numerous servants. The bond and the free were blended in Israel, a fact which also had its significance for the future, 1 Cor. xii. 13. The servants of Abraham are repeatedly spoken of, Gen. xii. 5, 16, xiii. 7, xx. 14, xxiv. 35; that these were possessed by him in great numbers, appears from his having 318, Gen. xiv. 14, who were trained, and whom he could arm. We also read of Isaac's herdmen, Gen. xxvi. 20, and of his 'great store of servants,' ver. 14. And while Jacob was still engaged with Laban, it is said, Gen. xxx. 43, 'The man increased exceedingly, and had much cattle, and *maid-servants* and *men-servants*, and camels, and asses.' Also, in his message to his brother Esau, he spake of his *men-servants* and his *women-servants*, xxxii. 5. Comp. ver. 7, 16. And the attack upon the city of Shechem by Simeon and Levi, xxxiv.

25–29, certainly was not made single-handed. Now when Jacob and his family took down into Egypt 'their flocks and their herds and *all that they had*,' xlv. 10, xlvii. 1, how can this possibly be understood otherwise than as including the servants which Jacob procured of his own, as well as those which he inherited from his father?

It is a mistake to overlook the fact that the patriarchs were really such. We must not conceive of them as wandering about with an insignificant household of two, three, or a dozen. They were heads of numerous and powerful communities. Abraham is addressed, Gen. xxiii. 6, as a 'mighty prince' (lit. *prince of God*); and he made a successful attack upon a band of pillaging invaders, avenging the injury done his kinsman, and driving them beyond the borders of the land, xiv. 14, etc. The king of the Philistines, whose army is incidentally mentioned, Gen. xxvi. 26, said to Isaac, 'Thou art much mightier than we,' ver. 16. Such, in fact, was the greatness of the patriarchal community, that Joseph could expect to be understood by an Egyptian when he called Canaan 'the land of the Hebrews,' Gen. xl. 15.

The analogy of collateral tribes or nations may further confirm the view which is here taken. Esau, when he met Jacob returning from Padan-Aram, was at the head of 400 men, Gen. xxxiii. 1. This was a part of the band which he had gathered around him, and from which the nation of Edom was derived. Accordingly, all his grandsons were dukes, xxxvi. 15, as the sons of Ishmael were princes, xxv. 16. And thus we read of 'a company of Ishmaelites' as early as the days of Jacob, xxxvii. 25.

Now, with these facts before us, what are we to say of the fitness of a man to comment upon the Pentateuch or its history who can talk in the following manner (p. 176).

It is offered in reply to a suggestion of Kurtz substantially agreeing with what has been said above.

"(i) There is no word or indication of any such a cortège having accompanied Jacob into Egypt.

"(ii) There is no sign even in Gen. xxxii, xxxiii, to which KURTZ refers, where Jacob meets with his brother Esau, of his having any such a body of servants.

"(iii) If he had had so many at his command, it is hardly likely that he would have sent his darling Joseph, at seventeen years of age, to go, all alone and unattended, wandering about upon the veldt in search of his brethren.

"(iv) These are also spoken of as 'feeding their flocks,' and seem to have had none of these 'thousands' with them, to witness their ill-treatment of their brother and report it to their father.

"(v) Nothing is said about any of these servants coming down with the sons of Jacob to buy corn in Egypt, on either of their expeditions.

"(vi) Rather, the whole story implies the contrary,—'they speedily took down every man his sack to the ground, and opened every man his sack,'—'then they rent their clothes, and laded every man his ass, and returned to the city,'—'we are brought in, that he may seek occasion against us, and take us for bondmen, and our *asses*,' not a word being said about *servants*.'

"(vii) In fact, *their eleven sacks* would have held but a very scanty supply of food for one year's consumption of so many starving 'thousands.'*

"(viii) The flocks and herds did not absolutely require any 'servants' to tend them, in the absence of Jacob's sons, since there remained at home, with the patriarch himself, his thirty-nine children and grand-children, as well as his sons' wives."

What has all this rigmarole to do with the subject, and how does it disprove one of the evidences already presented of the possession by Jacob of numerous servants? Because there is no express mention of servants in the

* So far from Joseph thinking that "eleven sacks" would answer for "one year's consumption," he sent 'ten asses laden with the good things of Egypt, and ten she-asses laden with corn and bread and meat for his father *by the way*,' Gen. xlv. 23,—just to support him during the journey down from Canaan; and this in addition to the provision specially given to his brethren for the like purpose, ver. 21.

two trips which Jacob's sons made into Egypt to buy corn, therefore they were unaccompanied by servants, therefore they possessed no servants! In 2 Chron. xxxvi. 6, 7, we read—

'Against him (Jehoiakim) came up Nebuchadnezzar king of Babylon, and bound him in fetters, to carry him to Babylon. Nebuchadnezzar also carried of the vessels of the house of the LORD to Babylon, and put them in his temple at Babylon.'

We suppose that the Bishop understands this passage to mean that Nebuchadnezzar came up alone, since there is no mention of any army, or even of any attendants, and that he personally fettered the king of Judah, and carried off the vessels of the house of the LORD.

These servants of the patriarchs were circumcised, Gen. xvii. 12, 13, and thus brought within the pale of the covenant. They were regarded as forming part of their household, vs. 23, 27, and were to be instructed to 'keep the way of the LORD,' Gen. xviii. 19. The circumcised stranger and the native Israelite were to be precisely on a par in all religious privileges, Ex. xii. 48, 49, Lev. xix. 33, 34, Num. ix. 14, xv. 14–16, Deut. xxix. 11. Under these circumstances, the distinction between the family proper and the household, between the children and servants of the patriarchs, would not be so broad as modern usages might lead us to imagine, and under the pressure of a common bondage, to which they were subjected in Egypt, might easily be done away altogether.

Strangers living apart in their independent households might attach themselves to the people of God. They were at liberty to embrace the covenant of Isráel, submit to its requisitions, and share its blessings, and were thenceforward reckoned as belonging to the seed of Abraham. 'Thou shalt not abhor an Edomite, for he is thy brother. Thou shalt not abhor an Egyptian, because thou wast a stranger in his land. The children that are begotten of them shall *enter into the congregation of the* LORD in their third generation,' Deut. xxiii. 7, 8. And it is remarked as a peculiar provision, based on special reasons, that 'an Ammonite or a Moabite shall not enter into the congregation of the LORD;' those also were excluded who had been guilty of idolatrous self-mutilation, Deut. xxiii. 1—3. This implies, of course, the possibility of admission in cases where there is no such express prohibition. The incorporation of other nations with Israel formed one of the standing objects of Messianic expectation, Isa. xiv. 1, lvi. 6–8, Ezek. xlvii. 22, Zech. viii. 23: it could not therefore have been contrary to their ancient and steadfast traditions. Now if these rights and privileges were accorded to foreigners generally, how much more to those who by their relation of service were already members of Israelitish households.

That the patriarchs and their descendants felt it to be no degradation to intermarry with their servants, appears from the case of Abraham and Hagar, and that of Jacob and his two maids, Bilhah and Zilpah. Marriages with servants and captives taken in war are distinctly contemplated and provided for in the law, Ex. xxi. 8–9, Deut. xx. 14, xxi. 11. Colenso supplies us with another fact in point, p. 167:

'In 1 Chron. ii. 34, 35, we read that Sheshan, a descendant of Judah in the ninth generation, 'had a servant, an Egyptian, whose name was Jarha; and Sheshan gave his daughter to Jarha his servant to wife, and she bare him Attai,' whose descendants are then traced down through twelve generations, and are reckoned, apparently, as Israelites of the tribe of Judah. From this it would seem that Hebrew girls might be married to foreigners,—we may suppose, proselytes,—and their children would then be reckoned as 'children of Israel.'"

Such marriages, not being regarded as objectionable at any time, would be still more likely to occur in Egypt, not only because the heavy hand of oppression was exerted to reduce master and servant to a level; but with whom else could they be contracted? Colenso puts the case in the following terms, pp. 164, 165, though with a very different design from that with which we quote his language.

"With the story of Isaac's and Esau's and Jacob's marriages before us, we cannot suppose that the wives of the sons of Jacob generally were mere heathens. Judah, indeed, took a Canaanitish woman for his wife or concubine, Gen. xxxviii. 2. But we must not infer that all the other brothers did likewise, since we find it noted as a special fact, that Simeon had, besides his other five sons, 'Shaul, the son of a Canaanitish woman,' Gen. xlvi. 10."

"But, however this may have been, we must suppose that in Egypt,—at all events, in their later days, for a hundred years or more, from the time that their afflictions began,—such friends [viz. their relations in Haran] were not accessible. We must conclude, then, that they either took as wives generally Egyptian heathen women, or else intermarried with one another. The former alternative is precluded by the whole tone and tenor of the narrative. As the object of the king was to keep down their numbers, it is not to be supposed that he would allow them to take wives freely from among his own people, or that the women of Egypt, (at least, those of the generation of Amram, which gave birth to Moses, and after it), would be willing generally to associate their lot with a people so abject and oppressed as the Hebrews."

In all probability long before the term of the Egyptian residence was reached, all distinction between the direct descendants of the patriarchs and their several retinues had ceased. The posterity of all blended together constituted the 600,000 men who went up out of Egypt under the leadership of Moses. So that the question in actual fact is not how could this enormous increase have arisen from 70 souls, but rather from several vast households of dependents and retainers, whose numbers we have no means of actually estimating.

It might be added to this that considerable numbers of the Egyptians may have attached themselves to Israel, not as "heathen," but won by the splendour of the promises made to the chosen seed, and the glorious prospects before them. This is quite as possible as that they should be deterred by their externally "abject and oppressed" condition. In fact we read of a 'mixed multitude,' Ex. xii. 38, Num. xi. 4, which went up with them. And mention is made Lev. xxiv. 10, of 'the son of an Israelitish woman, whose father was an Egyptian.' 1 Chron. iv. 18, speaks of 'Bithiah the daughter of Pharaoh,' as married to a man of Judah;* her very name, which signifies *daughter of Jehovah*, implies that she was a convert to the worship of the true God. Moses also married an Ethiopian woman, Num. xii. 1.

All this does not conflict with the language of Deut. x. 22, 'Thy fathers went down into Egypt with threescore and ten persons; and now the LORD thy God hath made thee as the stars of heaven for multitude.' Or with Heb. xi. 12, 'Therefore sprang there even of one, and him as good as dead, so many as the stars of the sky in multitude, and as the sand which is by the sea-shore innumerable.' It is obvious that such general and rhetorical statements are not to be pressed to the letter, any more than the figures which they contain are to be absolutely pressed. They must find their more precise

* The date of this event is uncertain. But its having taken place at any time is sufficient for the purpose for which it is here adduced.

explanation and limitation in the facts as presented in detail elsewhere; and some of these facts have been exhibited above. The lineal descendants of the patriarchs formed the nucleus about which their dependents gravitated, and gave form and character to the nation thus created. The whole composed 'the house of Israel,' and were included amongst 'the seed of Abraham' by the organic law upon which that seed was originally constituted, Gen. xvii. 9–14.

CHAPTER XVI.

THE DANITES AND LEVITES AT THE TIME OF THE EXODUS.

BUT if the increase of the entire people can be thus satisfactorily accounted for, how is it with the individual tribes?

"Dan in the first generation has *one* son, Hushim, Gen. xlvi. 23; and, that he had no more born to him in the land of Egypt, and, therefore, had *only* one son, appears from Num. xxvi. 42, where the sons of Dan consist of only one family. Hence we may reckon that in the fourth generation he would have had 27 warriors descended from him, instead of 62,700, as they are numbered in Num. ii. 26, increased to 64,400 in Num. xxvi. 43.

"In order to have had this number born to him, we must suppose that Dan's one son, and each of *his* sons and grandsons, must have had about 80 children of both sexes.

"We may observe also that the offspring of the *one* son of Dan, 62,700, is represented as nearly double that of the *ten* sons of Benjamin, 35,400, Num. ii. 23."

Dan may have had daughters whose descendants were reckoned as belonging to their brother's family. The same would have been the case if he had had other sons born to him in Egypt, for, as we saw in Chapter I., only those descendants of the patriarchs who were living at the time of the descent into Egypt had the right of giving names to families. The old fallacy about 'the fourth generation' is here repeated again. If Jacob's posterity could swell to upwards of 600,000, Dan's 62,700 need occasion no trouble.

The fact that the numbers of each tribe in the days of Moses do not preserve the proportion of the sons of the several patriarchs living at the time of the migration to Egypt, appears to Colenso to cast doubt upon the truth of the narrative. To our minds it is a strong confirmation of its truth. It shows that these numbers have not been artificially made up. If they had been, they would have been framed into a more exact correspondence. And yet, after all, there is no reason or probability in the expectation that the ratio existing in a dozen families 430 years ago (about the time when Columbus was born) would be preserved, or even approximated in their descendants to-day. This free variety is as accordant with nature and with the facts of observation as it is unlike fiction.

The following tabular statement of the descendants of Jacob may present the matter to the eye in a convenient form.

	Gen. xlvi. Sons and Grandsons.		Num. xxvi. Families.	Num. i. 1st Census.	Num. xxvi. 2d Census.
Reuben	4		4	46,500	43,730
Simeon	6		5	59,300	22,200
Levi	3		3	22,000*	23,000*
Judah	3 +	2	5	74,600	76,500
Issachar	4		4	54,400	64,300
Zebulun	3		3	57,400	60,500
Gad	7		7	45,650	40,500
Asher	4 +	2	5	41,500	53,400

* The Levites were numbered from a month old and upward, and are not included in the general summation of the children of Israel given in Num. i. 46, xxvi. 51. There were, as appears from Num. iv. 48, 8,580 between 30 and 50 years of age. The rest of the tribes were numbered from 20 years old and upward.

	Gen. xlvi. Sons and Grandsons.	Num. xxvi. Families.		Num. 1. 1st Census.	Num. xxvi. 2nd Census.
Joseph	2 viz.	Manasseh	8	32,200	52,700
		Ephraim	4	40,500	32,500
Benjamin	10		7	35,400	45,600
Dan	1		1	62,700	64,400
Naphtali	4		4	53,400	45,400
Total	51+4		60	625,550	624,730

A fresh ground of complaint is found in the genealogy of the three sons of Levi—Gershon, Kohath, Merari.

"(i) These three increased in the *second* (Amram's) generation to 8, (not to 9, as it would have been, if they had had each three sons on the average,) viz. the sons of *Kohath* 4, of *Gershon* 2, of *Merari* 2, Ex. vi. 17–19.

"(ii) The 4 sons of *Kohath* increased in the *third* (Aaron's) generation to 8, (not to 12,) viz. the sons of Amram (Moses and Aaron) 2, of Izhar 3, of Uzziel 3, Ex. vi. 20–22. If we now assume that the two sons of *Gershon*, and the two sons of *Merari* increased in the same proportion, that is, to 4 and 4 respectively, then all the male Levites of the *third* generation would have been 16.

"(iii) The two sons of Amram increased in the *fourth* (Eleazar's) generation to 6, viz. the sons of Aaron 4, (of whom, however, two died, Num. iii. 2, 4,) and of Moses 2. Assuming that all the 16 of the third generation increased in the same proportion, then all the male Levites of the generation of Eleazar would have been 48, or rather 44, if we omit the 4 sons of Aaron who were reckoned as Priests. Thus the whole number of Levites, who would be numbered at the first census, would be only 44, viz. 20 *Kohathites*, 2 *Gershonites*, 12 *Merarites*, instead of 8,580, as they are numbered in Num. iv. 48, viz. 2,750 *Kohathites*, 2,630 *Gershonites*, and 3,200 *Merarites*, v. 36, 40, 44."

The Bishop seems to have expected to find in the genealogies the name of every Israelite who was living at the time of the exodus. If the whole 8,580 are not put down in the genealogies, they could not have existed. Upon this principle we would be obliged to have a book as large or larger than a New York directory, simply to record the names of the people.

But again, Colenso himself shows us that these genealogies do not always aim at completeness, even in respect to those families which have a place in them.

"In Ex. vi., while the sons of Amram, Izhar, and Uzziel are mentioned, no sons are assigned to their brother Hebron. In Num. iii. 27, however, we read of 'the family of the Hebronites;' and, in 1 Chron. xxiii. 19, *four* sons of Hebron are mentioned.

"So in Ex. vi. 21, 22, the sons of Izhar are *three*, and the sons of Uzziel, *three*: but in 1 Chron. xxiii. 18, 20, Izhar has only *one* son, and Uzziel, *two*."

The subject seems to call for no additional remark, except that the fallacy of the 'fourth generation' is here again at the bottom of the calculation.

But the Bishop tries to "put the matter in another and yet stronger light," as follows:

"The Amramites, numbered as Levites in the fourth (Eleazar's) generation, were, as above, only two, viz. the two sons of Moses, the sons of Aaron being reckoned as Priests. Hence the rest of the Kohathites of this generation must have been made up of the descendants of Izhar and Uzziel, each of whom had *three* sons, Ex. vi. 21, 22. Consequently, since *all* the Kohathites of Eleazar's generation were numbered at 2,750, Num. iv. 36, it follows that these *six* men must have had between them, according to the Scripture story, 2,748 sons, and we must suppose about the same number of daughters!"*

We could have found a much stronger case for him than this. There were 8 families in the tribe of Manasseh, Num. xxvi. 29–34, numbering in all 52,700 men

* Another instance of bad faith, for it admits of no other explanation, is found on p. 179, where he represents Kurtz as "almost driven to despair in his attempts to get over this difficulty;" and adduces in proof a quotation, which, torn from its connection, might seem like a refusal to credit the Mosaic narrative on account of its incongruities, but which is really part of an argument exposing the absurdities of the opinion entertained by the Bishop that Moses belonged to the third generation from Levi.

over twenty years of age. Assuming that these were equal, or nearly so, each family, as, for example, that of the Hepherites, descended from Hepher, ver. 32, must have numbered about 6,587. Now, we only read of Hepher's having one son, viz. Zelophehad, ver. 33, xxvii. 1: and of him it is expressly said that he had no sons, but five daughters. Hence these *five* women, themselves daughters of a man who 'died in the wilderness,' Num. xxvii. 3, must have had between them, according to the Scripture story, 6,587 sons, who were upwards of twenty years old, and we must suppose about the same number of daughters! Clearly, arithmetic is a wonderful thing.

Such results are to sensible minds not a proof of the Bishop's theorem, but a *reductio ad absurdum*. They prove not that Moses has blundered in this egregious way, but simply that Moses and Aaron do not belong to the next generation from Amram, and that they did not compose the whole of his descendants; and so Zelophehad could not have been the immediate and only descendant of Hepher. The Bishop is simply mistaken as to the term of the residence in Egypt, and the number of generations there; that is all.

The cavil based on the fact that the tribe of Levi had increased but 1,000 in the interval of thirty-eight years, which elapsed between the first and second census, is as groundless as those which we have been considering. There is not a particle of proof for his assertion that Levi was not included in the curse pronounced on all the tribes, that the men who were upwards of twenty, on leaving Egypt, should die in the wilderness. He speaks of Eleazar as surviving Joshua, Josh. xxiv. 33, but we do not know that he was over the fatal age. Aaron himself was debarred from Canaan, like all the rest. Some of the tribes increased in the interval, others decreased, shewing the various severity of the plagues with which they were from time to time visited. While most of the tribes remained somewhere in the region of their original numbers, Manasseh increased from 32,200 to 52,700, that is 63⅝ per cent. in 38 years or 13¾ per cent. in 10 years. Inasmuch as "the population of England increases at the rate of about 23 per cent. in 10 years," this rate will not be esteemed exorbitant. On the other hand Simeon fell off from 59,300 to 22,200, showing what terrible ravages the pestilence had made there; as a prince of Simeon was prominent in the affair of Baal-peor, Num. xxv. 14, that tribe had doubtless suffered most severely in the plague, ver. 9, which shortly preceded the second census, xxvi. 1.

The chapter which we are reviewing, fitly closes with the following extraordinary paragraph:

> "What are we to say of the whole story of the Exodus, of the camping and marching of the Israelites, of their fighting with Amalek and Midian, of the 44 Levites slaying 3,000 of the children of Israel, Ex. xxxii. 28? . . . . How were the 20 Kohathites, the 12 Gershonites, and the 12 Merarites, to discharge the offices assigned to them in N. iii. iv., in carrying the Tabernacle and its vessels,—to do, in short, the work of 8,580 men, Num. iv. 48? What were these forty-four people, with the two Priests, and their families, to do with the forty-eight cities assigned to them, Num. xxxv. 7? How could the Tabernacle itself have been erected, when the silver spent upon it was contributed, as we are expressly told, by a poll-tax of half a skekel, Ex. xxxviii. 26, levied upon the whole body of 603,550 warriors, who did not exist?"

Is not this the climax of outrageous misrepresentation? Where does Moses say anything of 44 Levites, 20 Kohathites, etc., doing what is here imputed to them? It would be a no more serious distortion, if we were to substitute for *Colenso, Bishop of Natal,* the anagram *N. B. Choose fatall poison,* and argue from that the deleterious nature of the tenets which he has chosen to adopt, or which he offers to the choice of others.

CHAPTER XVII.

THE NUMBER OF PRIESTS AT THE EXODUS COMPARED WITH THEIR DUTIES, AND WITH THE PROVISION MADE FOR THEM.

THE chapter of Colenso, with the above heading, is a repetition of his old method already practised *ad nauseam* of framing a theory at variance with the possibilities of the case, and then representing the Mosaic narrative as incredible, because his superficially formed theory of its meaning is so. He finds that the priests at the time of the Exodus were too few to have offered the numerous sacrifices, and performed the other services enjoined by the ritual. Any other man, under these circumstances, would have felt it incumbent upon him to institute a careful scrutiny into the facts of the case, and ascertain by the help of all the hints which can be gathered, how the matter was really managed. But the Bishop is above all such investigations. He is ready with his conclusion: the Pentateuch is "unhistorical."

Upon this subject we commend the following considerations to candid readers:—

1. The ritual prescriptions of the Pentateuch are largely designed for the future. They were not intended, as their very nature shows in a multitude of cases, to

come into developed operation in the wilderness, but anticipate the time when the people should be settled in the peaceable and secure possession of Canaan. This is so plain that the Bishop himself admits it, p. 190.

"Then follow other directions, by which it is provided that the Priest should have also 'the best of the oil, and all the best of the wine, and of the wheat, the first fruits of them, which they shall offer unto Jehovah,' and 'whatsoever is first ripe in the land;' which laws we may suppose were intended only to be applied, *when the people had become settled on their farms in the land of Canaan*, as also the law, ver. 25–29, for their receiving also a tenth of the tithes of corn and wine and oil, which were to be given for the support of the Levites."

Again (on p. 188,) he refers to another case, in which, if he states the facts correctly, the same inference must be drawn, although the Bishop is of another mind.

"Turtle-doves or young pigeons are prescribed as a lighter and easier offering for the poor to bring; they are spoken of, therefore, as being *in abundance* and within the reach of every one. . . . . In the desert, it would have been equally impossible for the rich or poor to procure them."

Colenso infers that "such laws as these could not have been written by Moses, but must have been composed at a later age, when the people were already settled in Canaan, and the poor who could not afford a lamb could easily provide themselves with pigeons." We infer either that the Bishop is mistaken about the scarcity of pigeons in the wilderness, or that this provision of the law was not to take effect until the people were living where pigeons could be had.

Moses was giving law for the entire future. He had to contemplate the circumstances of the people, therefore, as they would be in time to come. The regulations, which were impossible in their present condition, could of course apply to the future only. Before we give our assent to the Bishop's conclusion, we would like him to show, that according to the Mosaic record, Aaron and his sons actually performed or were expected to perform impossibilities: and that the multitudinous prescriptions, with which it was beyond their power to comply, were intended to go into operation in the wilderness.

2. Not only the language of the law, as we have seen, but the statements of the history show that the wandering in the wilderness was a provisional period, in which some of even the most important of the requisitions of the ritual were in abeyance. Thus we learn from Josh. v. 4–7, that the rite of circumcision was suspended from the time the children of Israel left Egypt until they entered the promised land. As far as our present purpose is concerned it does not matter how this fundamental statute came to be set aside for such a length of time. It may be attributed to the defection and culpable neglect of the people, or to a divine judicial sentence which temporarily deprived those, who had broken God's covenant, of the possession of its outward seal, or to a divine leniency which suffered the pretermission of the rite in consequence of the inconvenience and hazards with which it would be attended in their frequent journeying. Upon every explanation the fact remains that one of the most essential rites of the Old Economy was wholly omitted in the wilderness.

The prophet, Amos, v. 25, 26, implies the infrequency of sacrifices in this period. 'Have ye offered unto me sacrifices and offerings in the wilderness forty years, O house of Israel?' The Bishop quotes this passage as showing "that in the prophet's view, at all events, such sacrifices were required and expected of them." Perhaps so, and perhaps not. Some able commentators have been of a different opinion, supposing that the prophet is drawing a contrast between the paucity of the sacrifices expected and received from their fathers during a period of signal divine interposition on their behalf, and the degeneracy of their sons, who, with all the multitude of their offerings, had nevertheless provoked the divine displeasure, and should suffer a signal judgment.

But if we admit, as we are well disposed to do, that "in the prophet's view such sacrifices were required and expected," it will be still more damaging to the Bishop's cause. For, in the first place, even though they might have been "required," they were not offered: and so all the difficulty arising from the supposed inability of the priests to attend to them ceases. And, in the second place, we have here an unequivocal testimony on the part of this prophet that the house of Israel was in the wilderness forty years, and that sacrifices and offerings were "required and expected" of them there. If this substantial fact is true, the Pentateuch cannot be false.

Indeed, when we consider the abundant and explicit references which both Amos and Hosea, not to speak of the other prophets, make to the Pentateuch, their appeals to the facts which it records as undeniably true, their allusions to its statutes as of binding force and as in actual operation, and their citations of its very language, we are obliged to confess that we have here a very strong argument both for the Mosaic composition and the divine authority of the first five books of the Bible. Hosea and Amos are not only the oldest of the prophets whose writings are preserved to us, but their ministry was directed to the apostate kingdom of the ten tribes. This kingdom had been in a state of hostility with Judah from the days of Rehoboam, the son of Solomon. The ten tribes were under the strongest possible temptation to deny and disown the Pentateuch, some of whose most stringent provisions they were by their idolatry and schism habitually disregarding. And yet, here we see from these prophets that the authority of the Pentateuch was acknowledged, and some of its regulations were still in existence among these apostates. If it was not of Mosaic origin, but had been concocted in Judah since the time of the schism, how came it to be accepted by the ten tribes, though it was derived from a hostile people, and its commands were directly in the face of their practice and their political interest? No hypothesis can account for this, except that the Pentateuch was so firmly credited to be the word of God when the schism occurred that its hold upon the people's minds could not be shaken.

And if so thorough a conviction of its truth and its divine authority existed in the days of Solomon, then it unquestionably is what it professes to be, the genuine production of Moses. It could not have been forged in the days of David, for that was too near the time of the schism for its real origin to have been forgotten or to have escaped the knowledge of those interested in exposing its falsity. It could not have been forged in the turbulent times of the Judges; that is the very last period to which any one would think of referring the origin of such a cumbrous and minute ceremonial system. It could not have been forged in the days of Joshua, for apart from the military character of the period, which would be equally unfavourable to the production of such a system and its imposition upon the people, that was too near the time of Moses; how could the volume gain credit when every adult person could have borne evidence to its falsity? There is no time between Solomon and Moses to which the origin of the Pentateuch can be referred. If its authority was undisputed then, in the time of Solomon, it is all that it claims to be.

3. The functions strictly belonging to the priests in the work of sacrifice were few and simple. The victim was slain by the offerer himself. It was prepared for the altar by the Levites. Other preliminaries are spoken of as committed to servants, 1 Sam. ii. 13–15. The strictly sacerdotal functions were sprinkling some of the blood, or applying it with the finger to the horns of the altar, and laying the prescribed pieces upon the altar fire; and the time which this would consume in the case of each sacrifice would be very brief indeed.

4. The priesthood was in a transition state in the time of Moses and Aaron. Sacrifices had previously been offered by every head of a family for his own household. The tribe of Levi was set apart by Moses for the sacred ministries of the tabernacle; and the family of Aaron for the priesthood. But while the regulations prescribed in the Pentateuch define what the permanent law was to be, may not the transition have been in some respects a gradual one, so far at least that the Levites who were accepted instead of the first born of all the people may have been temporarily allowed to aid the priests even in their proper functions, if they were at any time overburdened? This would certainly have some remarkable analogies in its favour. Thus, Solomon in the profusion of his sacrifices, finding the altar inadequate, did not hesitate to depart from the letter of ceremonial requirement by sanctifying another, 1 Kin. viii. 64, 2 Chron.

vii. 7. And on the occasion of the revived ritual zeal in the reign of Hezekiah, it is said, 2 Chron. xxix. 34, that 'the priests were too few;' 'wherefore their brethren, the Levites, did help them till the work was ended.' Compare 2 Chron. xxxi. 2.

The allegation that the provision made for the priests was out of all proportion to their numbers, also overlooks the fact that this was chiefly a prospective arrangement designed to secure the comfortable maintenance of the priests in all time to come, and especially when their numbers should have greatly increased.

In making the charge that the portions set apart from the offerings for the use of the priests were more than they could possibly consume, Colenso has also overlooked the facts that they were not compelled to eat any more than they desired, and that these things were to be partaken of not only by the 'three priests,' but also by their sons, and in some cases, by their daughters also, and their entire households; 'every one that is clean in thine house shall eat of it,' Num. xviii. 11;—and even by the Levites generally, as we read Deut. xviii. 1, 'The priests the Levites and all the tribe of Levi shall have no part nor inheritance with Israel; they shall eat the offerings of the LORD made by fire and his inheritance.'

Since the preceding pages were in type, we learn from the newspapers that the Bishop has, in a subsequent volume just issued, announced his discovery, that the Pentateuch was written by the prophet Samuel. What the Christian world has hitherto regarded as the work of Moses, turns out, it seems, in the light of his investigations to be a summary of ancient traditions compiled by Samuel for the religious benefit of his contemporaries.

It would have been wiser or the Bishop to have

adhered to the negative ground maintained in the volume which we have been reviewing. As long as he contented himself with merely finding fault with current opinions, without suggesting any substitute of his own, he put his antagonists on the defensive, and could select or vary his point of attack at pleasure. In venturing a positive assertion of his own, however, he foregoes this advantage and lays himself open to attack in turn. The question can immediately be raised, whether the view which he proposes possesses any advantage over that which has always been held—whether it may not be encumbered with difficulties quite as serious as that which we are requested to discard for its sake.

As we have not seen this second publication of Colenso, we do not know the precise form of the hypothesis which he adopts, nor the nature of the arguments upon which he professes to rest it. We are not sure, for example, whether he regards Samuel as the author of the entire Pentateuch in its present form, or as one of a series of writers amongst whom the dissecting processes of the German so-called higher criticism has parcelled it. In either case he has made a *faux pas*, and will have to guess again.

Having entered upon these studies so recently he may perhaps be pardoned for not knowing the risk he was running in venturing any assertion in the case. In fact the great trouble with that whole school of critics, whose humble disciple he has now become, is not in disproving the Mosaic origin of the Pentateuch. That is, upon their principles, an easy task. The Pentateuch cannot be the work of Moses, because in that case it would necessarily be a supernatural revelation, and a supernatural revelation is impossible. The case is prejudged, therefore, and the whole matter settled in advance. The real trouble is in knowing how to dispose of the Pentateuch after they have taken it away from Moses. They are in much the same predicament as the man, to whom some inconsiderate friend had made the present of an elephant; he had the animal on his hands and what in the world was he to do with it?

The Pentateuch is here. It must have originated at some time. It must have been written by somebody. The critics tell us that Moses was not its author, and that it was not composed in the Mosaic age. Very well. When, and by whom was it written? The propounding of this question raises a Babel-like confusion in the host where all seemed unanimity and harmony before. Nothing can be more hopeless and inextricable than the entanglements which are thus created. Theory has succeeded theory, and hypothesis followed hypothesis, until Milton's description of chaos seems to have been realized. Each phase of the subject lasts only till some fresh critic has had time to write a book, and substitute some new mystification of his own for that which had reigned previously. And the end is not yet. The difficulty is inherent in the subject. If the pyramids of Ghizeh be taken off of their base, it will require marvellous skill in engineering to balance them upon their apex. If the history of German critical hypotheses in relation to the Pentateuch has demonstrated any thing, it demonstrates that *no plausible and self-consistent theory can be framed of the origin of the Pentateuch, which denies its composition by Moses.*

As to this particular theory of the Bishop, which connects it with the name of Samuel, we cannot of course undertake its refutation in this place, for we have only a very indefinite notion of what the theory really is. He either thinks that Samuel was the author of the Pentateuch in its entire compass and in its present form, or that while Samuel wrote certain parts of it, its piecemeal composition was not brought to a close by him, and was not finally finished, perhaps, until long afterwards. In the latter case, the argument maintained above still stands. The Pentateuch in its present form and compass did not even upon the Bishop's theory originate in the interval between Solomon and Moses: and he will have to explain how it came to possess that consideration and authority in the kingdom of the ten tribes, which we learn from Amos and Hosea that it did possess.

If, however, Samuel was the author of the Pentateuch, as we now have it, he will have to explain:

1. How the traditions, of which this is supposed to be a record, could have originated and have been so firmly credited in Israel and by Samuel himself, if they are utterly untrue.

2. How a good man, as Samuel is supposed to have been, could have attempted to palm off a book which he prepared himself for the religious benefit of his contemporaries, as a production of the great Hebrew legislator, Deut. xxxi. 9, 24.

3. How he could succeed in making his contemporaries believe that a detailed history and an extensive code of laws produced by himself, had not only been in existence for ages, but had been the basis of their national constitution, and had all along been in the custody of the Priests to whom it was committed, and had been publicly read to themselves every seventh year, Deut. xxxi. 11.

4. How, after opposing the wishes of the people in

their desire to have a King and remonstrating with them upon its sin and its impropriety, 1 Sam. viii., he could write a book representing the founder of the Hebrew State contemplating without disapproval the establishment of a kingdom, Deut. xvii. 14–20.

5. How Samuel could be the author of a minute and extensive system of laws, the fundamental principle of which restricted the offering of sacrifices to the Aaronic priesthood and to the place of the sanctuary, and which made the ark of the covenant prominent as the centre of all religious service, when during nearly the whole of his life the ark was in obscurity, 1 Sam. vii. 1, 2; 2 Sam. vi. 4, and almost the only sacrifices of which we hear were offered by himself, though he was not descended from Aaron, 1 Sam. vii. 9, 10; viii. etc. etc., and these, moreover, were never offered at the Sanctuary.

CHAPTER XVIII.

THE PRIESTS AND THEIR DUTIES AT THE CELEBRATION OF THE PASSOVER.

NEXT follows an attempt, which if we might do so without disrespect, we would call a very clumsy one, to create a difficulty without even the semblance of a ground for it in the statements of Moses.

"We are told, 2 Chron. xxx. 16, xxxv. 11, that the people killed the Passover, but '*the Priests sprinkled the blood from their hands*, and the Levites flayed them.' Hence, when they kept the second passover under Sinai, Num. ix. 5, where we must suppose that 150,000 lambs were killed at one time 'between the two evenings,' Ex. xii. 6, for the two millions of people, each Priest must have had to sprinkle the blood of 50,000 lambs in about two hours, that is, at the rate of about *four hundred lambs every minute for two hours together.*"

Because seven or eight centuries afterwards, when the priests formed a numerous body, they had assumed the charge of the whole ceremonial, as far at least as they were capable of doing so, therefore the three priests of Aaron's days must have done the same in spite of the physical impossibility. And this impossibility of the Bishop's own getting up proves not that he is mistaken, but that Moses is "unhistorical." No further reply is necessary than is furnished by the admission (p. 202),

"It is certainly true that the references to the passover in the books of Exodus and Numbers, *do not appear to imply in any way* that the priests were called into action in the celebration of this feast."

The same remark applies likewise to the additional difficulty, which is pretended here, viz. that the court of the tabernacle did not afford space enough for the slaughtering of all the lambs which must have been slain at the passover.

"In the time of Hezekiah and Josiah, when it was desired to keep the Passover strictly, 'in such sort as it was written,' 2 Chron. xxx. 5, the lambs were manifestly killed *in the Court of the Temple.* We must suppose, then, that the Paschal lambs in the wilderness were killed *in the Court of the Tabernacle,* in accordance, in fact, with the strict injunctions of the Levitical Law, that all burnt-offerings, peace-offerings, sin-offerings, and trespass-offerings, should be killed 'before Jehovah,' at the door of the Tabernacle of the Congregation."

"But the area of that Court contained, as we have seen, only 1,692 square yards, and could only have held, when thronged, about 5,000 people. How then are we to conceive of 150,000 lambs being killed within it by, at least, 150,000 people, in the space of two hours,—that is, *at the rate of* 1,250 *lambs a minute?*"

The books of Moses do not say one word about the slaying of the passover lambs in the court of the tabernacle. No direction is given to that effect. No statement is made implying it. But, says our reasoner, Hezekiah and Josiah desired to keep the passover 'in such sort as it was written;' and the lambs were then killed in the court of the temple; therefore it must be written in the books of Moses, that they should be killed in the court of the tabernacle, although we have these books in our hands, and can see for ourselves that they contain nothing of the sort! Why does not the Bishop argue that the Mosaic passover must have been kept at Jerusalem, because Hezekiah and Josiah kept it 'as it was written,' and they kept it at Jerusalem? The Mosaic directions about the passover are contained Ex. xii. 1–28, and there is not one word about the tabernacle or the priests in the entire passage. Upon its second observance no new regulations were given; the people were simply referred to what had been enjoined upon them before. "Ye shall keep it in his appointed season; according to all the rites of it, and according to all the ceremonies thereof shall ye keep it," Num. ix. 3.

But in order to prove that the passover must be slain in the court of the tabernacle, and that its blood must be sprinkled by the priests, Colenso refers us to—

"this most solemn command laid down in Lev. xvii. 2–6, with the penalty of *death* attached for disobedience."

"This is the thing which the LORD hath commanded, saying, What man soever there be of the House of Israel, that *killeth* an ox, or *lamb*, or goat, in the Camp, or that killeth it out of the Camp, and *bringeth it not unto the door of the Tabernacle of the Congregation*, to offer an offering unto the LORD, before the tabernacle of the LORD, blood shall be imputed unto that man, he hath shed blood, and *that man shall be cut off from among his people;* to the end that the children of Israel may bring their sacrifices, which they offer in the open field, even that they may bring them unto the LORD, *unto the door of the Tabernacle of the Congregation, unto the Priest*, and offer them for peace-offerings unto the LORD. And *the Priest shall sprinkle the blood upon the Altar of the Lord, at the door of the Tabernacle of the Congregation*, and burn the fat for a sweet savour unto the LORD."

This quotation is neither pertinent to the question, nor is it honestly made. There is not the slightest allusion in it to the passover. The regulation prohibits sacrifices from being offered in the open field, or anywhere but at the prescribed place for sacrificial worship. It was designed to guard against the idolatry to which Israel was prone, and into which the people were already falling. Why does the Bishop seek to hide this from his readers by breaking off his quotation where he does, when the very next words would have shown that the statute has relation to a very different subject from that to which he applies it? The thing to be prevented is declared in ver. 7, 'And they shall no more offer their sacrifices unto idols, after whom they have gone a whoring.' What is there in this to intimate that the passover was to be observed differently from the law of its original institution, especially when this would have encumbered its observance with a physical impossibility?

We pass to the last count in the indictment.

CHAPTER XIX.

THE WAR ON MIDIAN.

BEFORE proceeding to the proper theme of this chapter, our author reviews his work with a gratified complacency; and in the course of this review, he indulges in a fling at "the extravagant statements of Hebrew writers," or the "systematic habit of exaggeration in respect of numbers, which prevails among Hebrew writers of history," and which he alleges to be "more especially true of the Chronicler."

We can scarcely be expected, at the close of this discussion, to enter thoroughly into the refutation of a random remark of this kind, which has no connection with the subject properly in hand. Nor do we deem it necessary to trouble either ourselves or our readers with a particular examination of the numbers taken from the books of Judges, Samuel, and Chronicles, upon which he professes to found it. He has presented no reasons for discrediting these numbers; they only appear to him to be too large. If our experience of his accuracy and reliability has not been such as to warrant our taking all his dicta upon trust, and if we are not willing to condemn the sacred writers upon bare suspicion and without investigation, we can scarcely renounce their authority so summarily as he would have us do. We would be obliged to institute a careful inquiry into the circumstances of each individual case, and compare them with other well authenticated cases of like description, in the ancient world, before we could have reliable data for testing the accuracy of the numbers in question. And even if this should result in our admission of a probable error in one or more of these cases, we would still further have to extend our investigation into the numbers of the Bible generally, before we could frame a certain and reliable theory as to the source of such errors, or at any rate before we could be justified in imputing them to a "systematic habit of exaggeration."

We have no intention of going into such a protracted disquisition at present. But since the author of the books of Chronicles has been singled out as especially obnoxious to the charge of systematic exaggeration, we may be indulged with a few remarks upon the subject.

1. The differences in numbers between the narrative in Chronicles and the parallel account in Samuel and Kings, have often been made an occasion of needless cavil. But it should be remembered that every difference does not establish a discrepancy. Thus in 2 Sam. xxiv. 24, it is said that David bought the threshing-floor of Araunah the Jebusite and the oxen for fifty shekels of silver. But 1 Chron. xxi. 25, detailing the same transaction, affirms that David gave for the place six hundred shekels of gold. This apparent conflict, however, is easily reconciled by observing that the one price was paid for the threshing-floor simply, the other for the entire place, including the whole of the future temple-area and probably all Mount Moriah.

2. In those comparatively few instances, in which there appears to be a real discrepancy, the author of

Chronicles is so far from a "systematic habit of exaggeration" that he not infrequently has the smaller instead of the larger number. Thus according to 2 Chron. ix. 25, Solomon had 4,000 stalls for horses, but according to 1 Kings iv. 26, he had 40,000. The Hachmonite, who was chief of David's captains, 'lifted up his spear against 300 slain by him at one time,' 1 Chron. xi. 11; in 2 Sam. xxiii. 8, he is said to have slain 800 at one time. Gad offered to David from the Lord a triple choice of evils; among them, according to 1 Chron. xxi. 12, was 3 years' famine; 2 Sam. xxiv. 13, has it 7 years.

3. There is sometimes reason to believe that the text of Chronicles has the correct numbers, even when they are larger than those which are found in the parallel histories. According to 2 Sam. viii. 4, David took from Hadad-ezer a thousand and seven hundred horsemen, and twenty thousand footmen; 1 Chron. xviii. 4 has it 1,000 chariots and 7,000 horsemen, and 20,000 footmen. Here the numbers are greater in Chronicles, and yet a better proportion is preserved between the different branches of the service. And hence the common opinion is that the correct statement is the one found in Chronicles. That this was the judgment of the translators of the authorized English version, appears from their having inserted in Samuel the word 'chariots' taken from the text of Chronicles, though they did not venture to make any change in the numbers. It thus becomes 1,000 chariots and 700 horsemen, making the horsemen inferior in number to the chariots, which is less probable than that there were 7,000 horsemen as stated in Chronicles. So in the numbering of the people by David, 1 Chron. xxi. 5 gives to Israel 1,100,000 and to Judah 470,000 men capable of bearing arms: according to 2 Sam

xxiv. 7 Israel had 800,000, and Judah 500,000. The number assigned to Judah in the two accounts does not differ materially, but that attributed to the remaining tribes is considerably larger in Chronicles. And yet the probability is in favour of the statement in the latter, because it seems more likely than that Judah was so nearly an equivalent for all the rest of the tribes as the numbers of Samuel would make it.

4. Where there is reason to believe that the number in the existing text of Chronicles is too large, a disposition to exaggerate cannot with any probability be imputed to the writer. One of the most remarkable cases of this sort occurs, as cited by the Bishop, "in 2 Chron. xiii. 3, where Abijah's force consisted of 400,000 and Jeroboam's of 800,000, and Judah slew Israel, ver. 17, 'with a great slaughter; so there fell down slain of Israel 500,000 chosen men.'" Now although it is quite likely that there were as many men, as is here stated, in the two kingdoms capable of bearing arms, it is not very credible that they could all have been brought into active service at one time. And at any rate the slaughter of 500,000 men on one side in a single engagement, or even in a whole campaign, is so enormous that we are forced to suspect that there must be some mistake in the numbers.

Again, "Asa's force consisted of 580,000 . . . 2 Chron. xiv. 8, Jehoshaphat's of 1,160,000 'besides those whom the king put in all the fenced cities throughout all Judah,' 2 Chron. xvii. 14–19." This is so much larger than the armies in the same kingdom were at other periods, and even than we can suppose to have been raised in a kingdom of the extent of Judah, that there is probably an error somewhere.

But if the writer was given to exaggerating beyond all bounds, and was tempted in these instances to do so in order to enhance the military power of Judah, how comes it to pass that he does so only in three instances? Why should Abijah's, Asa's, and Jehoshaphat's armies be set down at so high a figure, while no such monstrous bodies of troops are assigned to the pious Hezekiah, or even to David the most distinguished of the military monarchs of Israel? According to 1 Chron. xxvii. David, though he reigned over the undivided people, had but 288,000 men enrolled in his standing army; and these were not liable to be called out together at any one time but were distinguished into twelve divisions, each of which served but a month at a time.

5. The most remarkable instance of discrepancy in numbers in the entire Old Testament, is of such a nature as to demonstrate in the most conclusive manner, not only that this alleged disposition to exaggerate affords no satisfactory solution of the phenomenon in question, but that it is impossible that it should have existed; and further, that these discrepancies can by no possibility be imputed to the original writers, but must have been introduced in the course of subsequent transcription. In Ezra ii. and Nehemiah vii, we have two parallel accounts, or rather two copies of the same account of those who came up with Jerubbabel, Joshua, and others from the captivity. And yet with an agreement throughout, which shows that the two lists are identical in origin, there are the following differences:

		Ezra ii.		Nehemiah vii.	
The Children of Arah,		ver. 5	775	ver. 10	652.
"	" Pahath-Moab,	" 6	2,812	" 11	2,818.
"	" Zattu,	" 8	945	" 13	845.

	Ezra ii.		Nehemiah vii.	
The Children of Bani (Binnui),	ver. 10	642	ver. 15	648.
" " Bebai,	" 11	623	" 16	628.
" " Azgad,	" 12	1,222	" 17	2,322.
" " Adonikam,	" 13	666	" 18	667.
" " Bigvai,	" 14	2,056	" 19	2,067.
" " Adin,	" 15	454	" 20	655.
" " Bezai,	" 17	323	" 23	324.
" " Hashum,	" 19	223	" 22	328.
Bethlehem and Netophah,	" 21, 22	179	" 26	188.
Bethel and Ai,	" 28	223	" 32	123.
The Children of Magbish,	" 30	156		wanting.
Lod, Hadid and Oho,	" 33	725	" 37	721.
The Children of Senaah,	" 35	3,630	" 38	3,930.
" " Asaph,	" 41	128	" 44	148.
" " The Porters,	" 42	139	" 45	138.
" " Delaiah, etc.,	" 60	652	" 62	642.

According to both Ezra ii. 64, and Neh. vii. 66, 'the whole congregation together was 42,360;' and yet the total of the numbers given in detail by Ezra is only 29,818, and by Nehemiah, 31,089. The traditional explanation of these missing thousands is perhaps the true one, that they were citizens of the ten tribes, or persons whose genealogy could not be traced. But the discrepancies between the two accounts still remain. And yet we do not suppose, that Colenso himself would suspect the writer of either book of having intentionally falsified the numbers. They are just such errors as would naturally and almost unavoidably arise in the repeated transcription of such long lists of unfamiliar names and numbers. But the idea of systematic alteration for the purpose of exaggerating, or for any purpose whatever, is absolutely precluded.

6. The occurrence of this class of textual errors is very readily explained, if we assume with the majority of commentators, that numbers were originally not written

out in full, but were expressed by numerical signs or symbols, and probably by the letters of the alphabet, to which numerical values were attached. It is known that the Jews did use their letters in this way, not only because the modern Jews so employ them, but upon the Maccabean coins the dates are expressed by letters, and not by words. The Greeks made a similar use of their letters. And that this was not original with them, but was borrowed from the Phœnicians, from whom they received their alphabet, appears from the fact, that their letters so used correspond in value with those of the Hebrews and Semitic nations generally; and that those letters which were dropped in ordinary use as signs of sound were nevertheless retained as symbols of number. Now, as א means 1, and א̈ 1,000, ד 4, and ר 200, ה 5, and ת 400, כ 20, and נ 50, etc. etc., it is easy to see how a slight mistake in a letter would introduce a serious discrepancy in numbers. And it is well known how unreliable figures often are in modern printing and telegraphing in spite of all the pains which are taken to secure accuracy. How can it be thought surprising, then, that numerical errors should creep into the text of a book which was for ages dependent for its preservation upon manual transcription? The wonder rather is, that these errors should be of so rare occurrence, and of such an unimportant character as they are.

7. But further, even if the inspiration of the author of Chronicles were to be reduced to that low and modified form, in which some have been disposed to hold the doctrine, of merely securing the correctness of all that was distinctively religious, but not of vouching for the truth of what was merely historical, statistical, or scientific, the writer being in these, just as other men would be, left to

the exercise of his unaided faculties; or even if the rationalistic hypothesis were accepted out and out, and the inspiration of the writer were denied altogether, still the charge brought by Colenso would be absolutely incredible and indefensible. There is no book in the Bible, in which such constant appeals are made to collateral sources of information, as in Chronicles. At the close of each reign reference is made either to the public annals of the kingdom, or other extant histories contemporaneous with the events recorded, both as confirming the facts here stated and as containing much that is here merely alluded to or is omitted altogether. How could a writer, expecting or desiring that his work should be accepted as a genuine history of his nation, make appeals of this sort to pre-existing works within reach of his readers, and at the same time be guilty of wilful falsifications of the record, and even betray such a "systematic habit of exaggeration in respect of numbers" that a South-African bishop can detect him in it with no collateral aids whatever, by his simple skill in arithmetic? *Credat Colenso, non ego.*

This matter of the numbers of the sacred text, with which Colenso deals so flippantly, and so superficially, we have not scrupled to present thus broadly upon our pages. It is one of the most plausible objections, which those who deny the inspiration of the writers of Holy Scripture have to allege; and we have spread it out in its details in its full force much more strongly than Colenso seems to have dreamed that it was capable of being exhibited. And what does it amount to? Why, simply this, that in a very few of the books of the Old Testament, those, namely, which deal most largely in numbers, transcribers have made occasional mistakes in the figures; and this in matters which are of no sort of moment as regards even the general facts of the history, not to say the truths and doctrines of the divine revelation. A man, whose faith in the Bible as the word of God is disturbed by such a cause, would dispute the reality of all the charges in his shop-keeper's bill, because the clerk, in adding up one of the columns, has made the mistake of a cent. The very character of these numerical errors, and the mode in which they originated, further show that they are limited to this specific thing. They imply no general corruption or inaccuracy of the text; and none, in fact, exists. It may be affirmed in the most unqualified manner, that no work of antiquity has come down to us with its text so carefully preserved and with so many helps for its restoration and correction, even in the minutest matters, as the Scriptures.

But what chiefly shocks the Bishop's soul is the inhumanity of the massacre of Midian. And in view of this he expresses his thankfulness, which he expects will be shared by his readers, that his trenchant arguments have at length disposed of the credibility of the Pentateuch. The oppressive faith of centuries is dispelled, and mankind can now breathe freely, since Colenso has arisen.

"How thankful we must be, that we are no longer obliged to believe, as a matter of fact, of vital consequence to our eternal hope, the story related in Num. xxxi, where we are told that a force of 12,000 Israelites 'slew *all* the males of the Midianites, took captive *all* the females and children, seized *all* their cattle and flocks (72,000 oxen, 61,000 asses, 675,000 sheep), and *all* their goods, and burnt *all* their cities, and *all* their goodly castles,'—without the loss of a single man,—and then, by command of Moses, butchered in cold blood all the women and children, 'except all the women-children who have not known a man by lying with him.' These last the Israelites were to 'keep for themselves.'"

"The tragedy of Cawnpore, where 300 were butchered, would sink intc nothing compared with such a massacre, if indeed we were required tc believe it."

We do not know that it would relieve his mind in any degree, if we were to suggest to him that the nation of the Midianites was not exterminated notwithstanding. We find them strong enough at the time of Gideon to reduce Israel to subjection, Judges vi.

A human life is an unspeakably precious thing. To destroy the life even of a single human being, without just cause and without rightful authority, is an atrocious crime in the sight both of God and man. The whole civilized world shuddered at the barbarities practised at Cawnpore. And yet at that very time England was shedding far more blood than flowed in the streets of that wretched town. She was giving up the lives of her brave and gallant soldiers, and the world rang with admiration of their valour. She was mowing down by thousands the rebellious Sepoys, and the world confessed it just. To maintain the integrity of her empire, to preserve order and stable government, were ends for which England judged that lives might be sacrificed, in profusion even, if need be. The American people are engaged in a struggle at this hour for the maintenance of the government under which they have thus far prosperously lived, for the preservation of the institutions bequeathed to them by their fathers, for their national life and unity. Thousands and tens of thousands of valuable lives have been lost already. But the verdict of the nation still is that no expenditure of life or treasure is to be regarded beside the momentous issues at stake. It is the common judgment of mankind, that with all the value to be set upon life there are interests which are worth purchasing by its loss, even upon an extensive scale.

Nor must it be forgotten that life may be forfeited by crime, and may then be justly taken by competent authority. What would be thought of a man who should sum up the judicial executions in England, and then charge that such a number of persons had, by command of the courts, been "butchered in cold blood?"

Israel was the people of God. In the midst of abounding idolatry, immorality and crime, they were selected to be trained up with reference to the coming salvation. The germs of divine truth were implanted amongst them, that they might unfold themselves and in due time their ripened fruit be given to the world. To no other people is the human race so largely indebted. Egypt, Babylon, Greece, and Rome had each its work to do, in preparation for the present age. The products of these various forms of civilization were successively poured into the lap of mankind, and had their share in constituting those rich treasures of art and learning and law, of material wealth, and liberal culture, and stable, free and beneficent institutions, which the world now enjoys. But the moulding hand of Israel has had far more to do in determining the present state of the world than all others combined. The law has gone forth from Zion, and its controlling influence has been acknowledged by 'many people,' and 'strong nations afar off,' Mic. iv. 2, 3. The religion, which has come to us from Israel, is one of the most powerful and essential elements in our existing civilization. To it we owe our best institutions, our noblest and most expansive ideas, our public security, our social elevation, our domestic happiness. This religion is bringing the world back to God from its state of alienation. It opens the way for the perishing and the lost to everlasting blessedness.

The world-wide and immortal interests suspended upon the right conduct of this scheme of saving mercy, with which Israel was for the time identified, were such, that a land might well be cleared of its inhabitants for them to occupy it, if this was necessary for its full development, or its successful issue. The Sovereign Disposer of all events might here enjoin, what throughout the history of the world He has again and again permitted, that one nation should dispossess another of its seats, and occupy them as its own inheritance.

The seclusion of Israel from other nations, into whose idolatries they might be enticed, or whose example would prove infectious, was an important part of the plan pursued in the training of that people. And this rendered necessary the emptying of some land of its inhabitants, that they might be planted in it. This was not done, however, by an arbitrary decree, which might sweep off the innocent. Much less in the slaughter of the Midianites and the extermination of the Canaanites, do we see the brutal ferocity of savage tribes, led by blood-thirsty leaders. It was nothing of the sort. It was just the execution of a divine judicial sentence. He, who in the history of the world perpetually employs one nation as the unconscious instrument of his judgment upon another, here appointed Israel to be the conscious executioner of his just decree. The iniquity of the Amorites was at length full. They had sunk to a degree of debasement, execrated even in the Pagan world, and they were doomed by the Righteous Governor of all to be cut off.

The old dispensation was a period of law, administered

with rigour and strict severity. The idea of the sacredness and majesty of the divine law, the fearfulness of its sanctions, and the necessity of obedience, was the first thing to be inculcated. This was applied as sternly to Israel themselves as to others. The penalty of violating the law of God in a number of prescribed particulars was death; and even in less heinous instances, the only condition of pardon and restoration to theocratic privileges was the presentation of a bloody sacrifice. Blood must flow for sin, either that of the transgressor himself or of an accepted substitute. The murmurings and transgressions of the people in the wilderness were terribly avenged. Pestilence, fire from the Lord, and serpents taught the people fearful lessons of the sanctity of the law of God. And when the crime of the golden calf had been committed, the sons of Levi were directed, Ex. xxxii. 25, 'to put every man his sword by his side, and go in and out from gate to gate throughout the camp, and slay every man his brother, and every man his companion, and every man his neighbour.'

It was that they might gain a still deeper impression of the stern demands of inexorable law, that Israel was in this signal instance entrusted with the execution of that law upon others which they were daily instructed to apply to themselves. Midian had enticed the people to the abominable and disgusting rites of their idolatry. For their criminal yielding to this solicitation, direction was given to the judges to put every Israelite to death who was joined to Baal-peor, Num. xxv. 4. And a plague broke out in the camp which carried off 24,000, ver. 9. The Lord might have punished Midian, the principal and the instigator in this transgression, as he punished Israel, by a plague inflicted immediately by his own hand. And, we presume, that even Colenso would in that case have shrunk from arraigning the divine righteousness. He chose to make his people execute his sentence of destruction, that they might thus write their own condemnation in case they transgressed again themselves. The women were involved in the same sentence with the men, because they were equally guilty. Those only were spared, who were of too tender an age to have been involved in the crime or to prove a future source of contamination.

That Israel acted not as a people impelled by a savage thirst for blood and plunder, but as one conscious of their high commission, and doing the simple bidding of the Supreme, is apparent from their conduct at the taking of Jericho, where none of the spoils were appropriated by the people save the single theft of Achan, but all went into the treasury of the Lord. A people possessing such manifest tokens of the divine presence, and acting under God's immediate orders so confirmed, must not be confounded with one acting under a furious and fanatical zeal, and converting its own fancies and lawless propensities into imaginary divine ordinances. A people led by the pillar and the cloud, conducted through the Red Sea and the Jordan, and miraculously supported in the wilderness, was not a horde of fanatics. And a people which received its institutions from the flaming summit of Sinai, and which was for forty years instructed by a divinely appointed legislator, was not a lawless body of savages.

Colenso's further objection to the narrative, that time is not allowed for all the transactions recorded, scarcely needs an answer. It is based on a double assumption: First, that all the transactions were successive, and none of them contemporaneous; and, Secondly, that each of them must have occupied the length of time, which he arbitrarily assigns to it. As neither of these assumptions is capable of proof, the objection amounts to nothing.

CONCLUDING REMARKS.

We have now reached the end of our task. We have gone through the whole of what Colenso has to adduce against the credibility and authority of the Pentateuch. And we cannot help exclaiming, Is it for this that he would have us give up our faith in the Bible? Is it for this that he has abandoned his own?

As we write these lines we learn that another book of his has made its appearance, which is represented to be more open and virulent in its assault upon the Scriptures than that which we have now reviewed. We pity the man from our heart. We fear that never having had any thorough, well-grounded religious convictions, he has now made utter and hopeless shipwreck of the faith. He would appear to have so encircled himself with his miserable sophisms, as to have lost even the conception of the possibility of an honest and intelligent faith in others. To his disordered brain every thing is reeling, and he fancies every one else to be as unstable as himself. He has no idea but that bishops and clergy and churchmen are all secretly cherishing the doubts, which he alone has had the courage and the honesty openly to express.

We do not know what Colenso may have said in his new book and we do not care. Our aim is answered as completely by what we have now done, as if he had written a thousand books and we had answered them all. We have shown, we believe, his utter incapacity to deal with the questions which he professes to handle. We have spent no epithets upon him. We have uttered no denunciation. We have simply examined his statements and his arguments: and if such a fact is capable of demonstration, we have demonstrated that he has neither the candour, the learning, nor the ability to discuss the topics which he has undertaken to treat and upon which he pronounces so oracularly.

We have but a single remark to add: and that is, that Colenso grievously deceives himself as to the consequences which result from his position. He imagines that he can give up all faith in the historical truth of the Bible, all faith in it as a direct revelation from God, and yet that the religion of the Bible may remain in its integrity and power. There never was a greater mistake. Undermine the truth and the divine authority of the Scriptures, and everything is gone. If the Scriptures are not an infallible communication from God, but a mere record of the religious convictions of fallible men, and the truth or the falsity of whatever they contain must be judged of by "the voice of truth within" our hearts, then indeed we are reduced to a most miserable plight. Everything is involved in doubt, and uncertainty, and darkness.

Colenso tells us "that we *must* all, and we *may* all, depend entirely on our Father's mercy and come as children to his footstool continually for light and life, for help and blessing, for counsel and guidance." So we may, if the Scriptures are the very word of God. But if they are not, who can assure us of all this? Who can tell us whether this awful and mysterious silence, in which the Infinite One has wrapped himself, portends mercy or wrath? Who can say to the troubled conscience, whether He, whose laws in nature are inflexible and remorseless, will pardon sin? Who can answer the anxious inquiry whether the dying live on or whether they cease to be? Is there a future state? And if so, what is the nature of that untried condition of being? If there be immortal happiness, how can I attain it? If there be an everlasting woe, how can it be escaped? Let the reader close his Bible and ask himself seriously what he knows upon these momentous questions apart from its teachings. What solid foundation has he to rest upon in regard to matters, which so absolutely transcend all earthly experience, and are so entirely out of the reach of our unassisted faculties? A man of facile faith may perhaps delude himself into the belief of what he wishes to believe. He may thus take upon trust God's unlimited mercy, his ready forgiveness of transgressors, and eternal happiness after death. But this is all a dream. He knows nothing, he can know nothing about it, except by direct revelation from heaven.

The question, therefore, is one of life or death. We will not, we can not give up our faith in the Bible. To do so is to surrender ourselves to blank despair. It is to blot out the sun from the heavens and extinguish at once the very source of light and life and holiness. 'All flesh is as grass, and all the glory of man as the flower of grass. The grass withereth and the flower thereof falleth away; but the WORD OF THE LORD endureth forever.' 'Search the SCRIPTURES; for in them ye think ye have eternal life; and they are they which testify of me.'

THE END.

teacher, and the grammar of Gesenius has been a terrible stumbling-block to me. This grammar, a few years earlier, would have saved me endless perplexities, and encouraged and aided me not a little in the study of the language."—LYMAN COLEMAN, D.D., *Lafayette College.*

"That there is room for a better, more practical Hebrew Grammar all admit. That Prof. Green has made it, we are induced to believe. Though experience only can show this conclusively, yet we are disposed to think that Prof. Green has caught the right view of a Hebrew Grammar and carried it out with skill."—*The Presbyterian Quarterly Review.*

"This Grammar now under consideration is highly creditable to American scholarship, in the department of sacred literature, and we hail its appearance with pleasure."—*The Bibliotheca Sacra.*

"But is there really need of another Hebrew Grammar? With our by-gone recollections of Stuart and Nordheimer, we should say emphatically that there is." "At the instance of the late Prof. J. Addison Alexander, Prof. Green has undertaken to supply this deficiency—a work for which his learning in Oriental tongues and his experience in teaching, abundantly qualifies him. This grammar has already been adopted at several Seminaries."—*The New York Independent.*

"Dr. Green's Hebrew Grammar is a valuable addition to our Hebrew Literature."—WM. H. CAMPBELL, D.D., *New Brunswick.*

"While Prof. Green has made thorough use of the labors of other scholars, he has handled his materials in an independent manner, and produced a work which has a character of its own. We are sure that this grammar of Prof. Green's will be received with gratitude by biblical scholars, and justly valued as an important help to a more thorough knowledge of the old Testament Scriptures."—PROF. HENRY H. HADLEY, *Union Theological Seminary, New York.*

"I fully concur with what is said by Prof. Hadley in commendation of Prof. Green's grammar, with the plan and execution of which, so far as I have had opportunity to examine it, I am much pleased."—PROF. W. D. WHITNEY, *Yale College.*

"Prof. Green has united in an extraordinary degree simplicity with thoroughness, so that his grammar may be used at every stage of Hebrew study. The work has copious and well arranged indexes, four in number. It is altogether executed in a manner which reflects the highest honor on Biblical Science in America. We are acquainted with no Hebrew Grammar, which we can recommend so unreservedly as we can recommend this."—*The Lutheran and Missionary.*

"Prof. Green, of the Princeton Theological Seminary, has prepared an excellent Hebrew Grammar, which will doubtless come into very general use. The whole work is in a high degree creditable to American scholarship."—*American Theological Review.*

IN PRESS.

A HEBREW CHRESTOMATHY.

BY

WILLIAM HENRY GREEN,

PROFESSOR IN THE THEOLOGICAL SEMINARY, PRINCETON, N. J.

This work is a sequel to the Grammar of the author, and is designed to facilitate the progress of beginners in the Hebrew Language. It consists of a series of Grammatical Exercises and of selected portions from the Old Testament. The latter have been so chosen as to embrace many of the most interesting and important passages of the Hebrew Bible, of progressive difficulty and representing every variety of style· and they fully equal the amount read in our best Theological Seminaries in the course of the first year. They are accompanied by copious and carefully prepared Grammatical and Exegetical Notes and a Vocabulary.

VALUABLE TEXT-BOOKS, &c.,

PUBLISHED BY

JOHN WILEY, 56 WALKER ST., N.Y

MAHAN (PROF. D. H., LL.D.) AN ELEMENTARY COURSE OF CIVIL ENGINEERING FOR THE USE OF THE CADETS OF THE U. S. MILITARY ACADEMY. 1 vol. 8vo., with numerous wood-cuts. New Edition, with large Addenda, &c. Full cloth $3 50

"This work is used as the text-book on this subject in the U. S. Military Academy. It is designed also for use in other institutions. The body of the work is confined to a succinct statement of the facts and principles of each subject contained in it. The Appendix consists of the mathematical demonstrations of principles found in the text, with Notes on any new facts that from time to time appear."

MAHAN (PROF. D. H., LL.D.) A TREATISE ON FIELD FORTIFICATIONS; containing Instructions on the Methods of Laying Out, Constructing, Defending, and Attacking Intrenchments. With the General Outlines, also, of the Arrangement, the Attack, and Defence, of Permanent Fortifications. Third Edition, revised and enlarged. 1 vol. Full cloth, with steel plates 1 25

"This work is the text-book on this subject used in the U. S. Military Academy. It is also designed as a practical work for Officers, to be used in the field in planning and throwing up intrenchments."

MAHAN (PROF. D. H., LL.D.) AN ELEMENTARY TREATISE ON ADVANCED GUARD, OUT-POST, AND DETACHMENT SERVICE OF TROOPS, and the Manner of Posting and Handling them in the Presence of an Enemy. With a Historical Sketch of the Rise and Progress of Tactics, &c. &c., intended as a Supplement to the System of Tactics adopted for the Military Service of the United States, and especially for the use of Officers of Militia and Volunteers. 1 vol. 18mo. Full cloth 1 25

"This little work is designed to supply to some extent a want much felt among Officers in the outset of their duties, by pointing out to them the more usual rules for posting and handling troops in the daily services of a campaign."

MAHAN (PROF. D. H., LL.D.) INDUSTRIAL DRAWING; Comprising the Description and Uses of Drawing Instruments, the Construction of Plane Figures, the Projections and Sections of Geometrical Solids, Architectural Elements, Mechanism, and Topographical Drawing; with Remarks on the Method of Teaching the Subject. For the use of Academies and Common Schools. 1 vol. 8vo., twenty steel plates. Full cloth 2 50

"The design of this work is to teach Geometrical Drawing, as applicable to all industrial pursuits, in a simple, practical manner, to persons even who have made no attainments in Elementary Mathematics. For this purpose the method recommended is the oral one, in which each operation will be performed by the Teacher before the eyes of the pupil, by whom in turn it will be repeated. It is hoped that the work will also be found useful to all who are preparing themselves for any of the industrial pursuits in which Geometrical Drawing is required."

MOSELEY'S MECHANICAL PRINCIPLES OF ENGINEERING AND ARCHITECTURE. From last London Edition, with considerable additions, by Prof. D. H. Mahan, LL.D., of the U. S. Military Academy. 1 vol. 8vo., 700 pages, with numerous cuts. Cloth 4 00

FAIRBAIRN (WM.) C.E., F.R.S., ETC. ON THE APPLICATION OF CAST AND WROUGHT IRON TO BUILDING PURPOSES. 1 vol. 8vo. Numerous cuts. Cloth 2 00

"No engineer can do without this book."—*Scientific American.*

HATFIELD. THE AMERICAN HOUSE CARPENTER: A Treatise upon Architecture, Cornices and Mouldings, Framings, Doors, Windows, and Stairs, together with the most important Principles of Practical Geometry. Fifth Edition. 300 engravings. 8vo. Cloth 3 00

SMITH (LIEUT. R. S.) A MANUAL OF TOPOGRAPHICAL DRAWING. By Lieut. R. S. Smith, U. S. Army, Professor of Drawing in the U. S. Military Academy, West Point. 1 vol. 8vo. Plates. Cloth 1 50

"We regard the work as a choice addition to the library of science and art, and one that has long been needed by the Profession."—*R. R. Journal.*

CHEEVER'S WORKS, &c.

CHEEVER (REV GEORGE B.) WANDERINGS OF A PILGRIM IN THE ALPS. Part I.—In the Shadow of Mont Blanc. Part II.—In the Shadow of the Jungfrau Alps. In 1 vol. Cloth 1 00

CHEEVER (REV. GEORGE B.) THE JOURNAL OF THE PILGRIMS AT PLYMOUTH, IN 1620. Reprinted from the Original Volume; with Historical and Local Illustrations of Providences, Principles, and Persons. 1 vol. 12mo., uniform with the above. Cloth 1 0

CHEEVER (REV. GEORGE B.) The same. Cloth gilt 1 50

CHEEVER (REV. GEORGE B.) A DEFENCE OF CAPITAL PUNISHMENT. New edition. 1 vol. 12mo. Cloth, uniform with the above 50

CHEEVER (REV. GEORGE B.) THE HILL DIFFICULTY, and some Experiences of Life in the Plains of Ease. With other Miscellanies. Part 1.—Allegorical and Imaginative. Part 2.—Descriptive and Meditative. Part 3.—Critical and Speculative. 1 vol. 12mo. Cloth, with Steel Portrait of the Author 1 00

CHEEVER (REV. GEORGE B.) The same. Cloth, extra . . . 1 50

CHEEVER (REV. GEORGE B.) WINDINGS OF THE WATERS OF THE RIVER OF LIFE, in the Development, Discipline, and Fruits of Faith . . . 1 00

CHEEVER (REV. GEORGE B.) The same. Cloth, extra 1 50

"There is an exuberance of fancy, a peculiar glow, in the language of Dr. Cheever, which gives a charm to his written productions possessed by few."—*Com. Adv.*

ALEXANDER (PROF. J. A.) ON THE PROPHECIES OF ISAIAH. 2 vols. royal 8vo. Cloth. . . . .

ALEXANDER (PROF. J. A.) ISAIAH ILLUSTRATED AND EXPLAINED. An Abridgment of the Author's Critical Commentary on Isaiah. 2 vols. 12mo. Full cloth 3 00

"A rich contribution of philological exposition for the use of the clergy." —*Presbyterian.*

ATHEISTS—VOLTAIRE AND ROUSSEAU AGAINST THEM; or, Essays and Detached Passages from those writers, in relation to the Being and Attributes of God. Selected and Translated by J. Akerly. 12mo. Cloth 50

BEECHER (REV. EDWARD, D.D.) BAPTISM; with reference to its Import and Modes. 1 vol. 12mo. Cloth 1 25

BIBLIOTHECA SACRA AND THEOLOGICAL REVIEW. Conducted by Profs. Park, Taylor, Robinson, etc. Published quarterly. Per annum . . 4 00

BUSH (PROF. GEO.) ANASTASIS ON THE DOCTRINE OF THE BODY NATURAL AND SCRIPTURALLY CONSIDERED. Second edition. 1 vol. 12mo. Cloth . . . .

HEIGHWAY (O. T.) LEILA ADA, THE JEWISH CONVERT. An authentic Memoir. Including also her Diary. By O. T. Heighway. 1 vol. 18mo. Cloth. Second edition 75

"One of the most touching and remarkable portraitures we ever read."—*New York Evangelist.*

HEIGHWAY (O. T.) THE RELATIVES OF LEILA ADA. With some Account of the Present Persecutions of the Jews. 1 vol. small 12mo. Cloth 65

PRINCETON ESSAYS, THEOLOGICAL AND MISCELLANEOUS. Reprinted from the Princeton Review (including the Contributions of the late Rev. Albert B. Dod). Second Series. 8vo. Cloth . . . .

PRINCETON ESSAYS. THEOLOGICAL AND MISCELLANEOUS. First Series. London edition. 8vo. . . . .

ROBINSON (REV. DR.) BIBLIOTHECA SACRA. Tracts and Essays on Topics connected with Biblical Literature and Theology. Complete in 1 vol. 8vo. Cloth . 8 00

ROBINSON (REV DR.) The same. Separate numbers, each 1 00

DOWNING'S WORKS, &c.

DOWNING (A. J.) COTTAGE RESIDENCES; or, a Series of Designs for Rural Cottages and Cottage Villas, and their Gardens and Grounds, adapted to North America. Illustrated by numerous engravings. Third edition. 8vo. Cloth . . . 2 50

"Here are pleasant precepts suited to every scale of fortune among us; and general maxims which may be studied with almost equal profit by the householder in the crowded city, and the man of taste who retires with a full purse to embody his own ideas of a rural home."

www.ingramcontent.com/pod-product-compliance
Lightning Source LLC
LaVergne TN
LVHW011218110826
845150LV00006B/1461

* 9 7 8 1 4 2 5 5 1 7 0 4 5 *